I0026756

DO IT WRITE

NICOLA MARSH

Copyright © Nicola Marsh 2013
Published by Parlance Press 2022
Latest edition published by Nicola Marsh 2022

All the characters in this book have no existence outside the imagination of
the author and have no relation whatsoever to anyone bearing the same
name or names. They're not distantly inspired by any individual known or
unknown to the author and all the incidents in the book are pure invention.

All rights reserved including the right of reproduction in any form. The text
or any part of the publication may not be reproduced or transmitted in any
form without the written permission of the publisher.

For multi-award winning and USA TODAY bestseller Nicola Marsh, writing is a passion, an obsession.

In this jargon-free reference, she explores various writing tips for publication and beyond: stellar settings, the first 5 pages, what drives your story, motivation, editing, speed writing, methodology, revisions, resilience and more, including sample synopses.

This concise writing guide, with its tips and examples, will spark the imagination and help the words to flow.

FOREWORD

If you're anything like me, writing is a passion.

A necessity.

An obsession.

When I'm not writing, I'm a tad grumpy. (Or maybe that's the chocolate deprivation once I've made deadline?)

Writing keeps me centered and focused and grounded in a way that nothing else can.

And when I'm not physically writing, I'm mentally plotting or storing snippets to create characters later. Or feeding my stationary addiction by buying way too many gorgeous hardcover notebooks for the 'Next Great Idea.'

There are many writing 'how-to' reference resources. I have some wonderful 'how-to' books on my shelf and constantly save articles that resonate from the Internet.

Only one problem: the actual mechanics of writing intimidates me.

Story arcs, plot points, turning points, scene and sequels, etc.... are all fabulous ways to foster writing but if I try to apply the mechanics to my writing, my creativity freezes.

That's not what I want to happen when you read this book.

Sure, I've included some intrinsic 'how-to' stuff like character interview questions and sample synopses, but much of what is between these pages is personal experience garnered from twenty years in the publishing industry.

I hope some chapters will resonate more than others. As will the tips to get published and hints of how to handle it once you achieve your dream.

Publishing is an ever-evolving industry that morphs and grows.

It's an incredibly exciting time to be a writer.

I hope some of my insights help you on the wild, exhilarating ride from blank page to publication...and beyond.

WHAT DRIVES YOUR STORY?

About five years into my writing career, I had an interesting chat with my editor at the time. She pointed out that my books were plot driven and she wanted me to try a character driven book.

O-kay...so what did I do?

Firstly, I sat down and analyzed how I'd written my previous 16 books.

The first few were magical, stories that flew from my fingertips because once I discovered I could write I couldn't stop. Then the writing caper got a harder. I had deadlines. Series guidelines. Mini-series within a series.

So I started to plot: fill in a basic character sheet for hero/heroine, write an outline, describe the key scenes in a sentence or two, even describe each chapter with a sentence or two.

Once I wrote a few books like this, I become more of a pantser, following a basic outline but going where the characters took me. If I got stuck, it was back to trusty pen and paper to jot down those key scenes and off I'd go again.

See a theme emerging? I was focused on the scene, on

the plot, on making the story happen. Sure, the characters were there, happily doing their thing but I didn't ever interview my characters beforehand or really get to know them in-depth before starting the book. I just winged it. And when I really thought about it, the first thing that always came to me before I started writing a story was the plot: an interesting premise, a twist on the usual.

For my first book, I read an article on speed dating and thought 'wow, great idea for a story'. For my third book, Flirtatious, I wanted a butler story with a twist, so placed a princess on the run working as a butler for a CEO. For Hot Proposal, a twist on a reunion romance with first loves pitted against each other.

Each of these books, as with most of mine, the plot leapt to my mind first then the characters followed.

So with my editor's advice ringing in my ears, I chose a different approach.

I deliberately turned my back on plot and allowed my mind to wander, to focus on character, to allow a hero and heroine to come to me in a vague, wishy-washy kind of way before crystallizing.

To this end, I spent a month researching characterization on the Internet. Hours of checking out resources, reading articles, scanning character charts, delving into enneagrams, immersing myself in all things character.

Then I chose the resources best suited to me and devised my own brief character interview. Here are the questions I now answer before starting a book:

- **Character's greatest fear.... and why?**
- **What is the worst thing that could happen to him/her?**
- **Character is most at ease when:**

- **Most ill at ease when:**
- **Biggest vulnerability:**
- **Drives and motivations:**
- **Talents:**
- **Character flaws:**
- **Mannerisms:**
- **Biggest accomplishment:**
- **Character's darkest secret:**
- **Does anyone else know?**
- **If yes, did character tell them?**
- **If no, how did they find out?**

There are plenty of character profile worksheets available, asking a staggering array of questions. I stick to the key questions above.

In effect, I interviewed my hero and heroine before delving into plot. The other vital things I needed to know about my characters were:

- **What does she think she wants? (External goal)**
- **What does she really want? (Internal goal)**
- **Why does she want it? (Her motivation)**
- **What's her problem when the story starts?**
- **How will it get worse?**

(Applied to the hero too.)

Once I answered these questions, I knew my characters. I knew what drives them, how they'd react in a situation, what they really wanted. Only then did I let myself choose a plot suited to these two characters.

The result? I choked up for the first time when writing a book and I made my new editor cry, twice (in a good way!)

Rich characters are one of the keys to a great book: characters that make you cheer for them, characters that draw you into the story, vibrant, realistic characters that make you sigh with regret when you close the book.

You need to make your characters come alive and one of the best ways to do this is know them intimately before you start writing the story.

So what drives your story? Why not try a character interview before you start the next one and find out?

THE FIRST 5 PAGES

Editors and agents read thousands of manuscripts a year and if you ask many of them, unless the first page doesn't hook them, let alone the first five, they won't read on.

So how do you make your first 5 pages memorable?

A KILLER FIRST LINE

I'm a sucker for a killer first line. It's a great hook to launch the reader into the rest of the story.

So how do you do it?

-Raise a question

-Introduce something unique/different

-Reveal something unanticipated

-Show something is about to change

Here are a few of my first lines to give you examples:

Families can be toxic. (MY SISTER'S HUSBAND)

Have you ever done something so terrible, so horrific, that it haunts you? (THE SCANDAL)

Hatred is a living, breathing entity. (THE LAST WIFE)

"I have a severe case of blue balls." (DID NOT FINISH)

Jess Harper was the first to admit, sex made her uncomfortable. (BRASH)

Look up stupid *in the dictionary and you'll find my picture.* (FAKING IT)

Beck Blackwood could kill them. (NOT THE MARRYING KIND)

"You should do him." (CROSSING THE LINE)

Jett Alcott knew lingerie. (WICKED HEAT)

"Come in and take off your clothes." (DATE ME)

Each of these opening lines raises questions.

-All families? Whose family?

-Who did something bad?

-Who hates that much?

-Is the rest of the book this irreverent?

-Why did sex make Jess uncomfortable? In a metaphorical or physical sense?

-Who does Beck want to kill and why?

-Why is Jett, a guy, an expert in lingerie?

-Who is being asked to take off their clothes and why?

Making your reader curious right from the start will tempt them to keep turning pages to find out answers to questions, and that's what you want: to create a page-turner.

CREATE SYMPATHETIC CHARACTERS

Not all characters you create have to be 'sympathetic' or likeable, but you need your reader to *relate* to the character so they'll continue to read the story.

Though many books deviate from this, introducing the main character in the first scene, making your reader care what happens to him/her, is a way to keep the reader hooked.

Introduce main conflict: While the first line will hook your reader, it's the main conflict that keeps the reader turning pages.

Try to hint at the main conflict in the first 5 pages: a threat to the main character, an inner turmoil, something that makes the reader care.

Painting a picture: May sound obvious but the first few pages should convey the general tone of the story. Try to give a sense of where the story is taking place without listing facts like a travelogue.

What not to do:

Avoid info dumping.

Avoid boring your reader with backstory.

Avoid excessive description (scenery, setting, world building.)

When you submit your manuscript, you only have a few seconds, a few minutes if you're lucky, to grab an editor's/agent's attention.

Make your first 5 pages sparkle and you'll definitely have them wanting to read more.

THE QUESTION YOU MUST ANSWER

We've all heard the terms 'premise' and 'theme' bandied around.

And if you're anything like me, having to label my story freaks me out.

If I had to do it, I'd say many of my contemporary romances are second chance stories.

But there's something more important than figuring out theme while you're writing. Answering the all-important **STORY QUESTION**.

What is a story question?

It's the question that drives a reader to finish the book or watch a movie.

Eg. Will Katniss Everdeen survive the Hunger Games?

Interestingly, the answer to the question isn't often in doubt.

We know Katniss will somehow outsmart her enemies and live.

But what's important is getting your reader to ***care*** about the story question.

And to do this, we need to get our readers to care about our characters.

Katniss provides for her sister Prim and her mother. She's their family's primary caregiver. She's resourceful and intelligent and fiercely protective. So protective she would rather sacrifice her life than that of Prim. But if she dies, who will look after her family? So she does whatever it takes to survive the Hunger Games and that makes her character more compelling.

Along with getting your reader to care about your characters, your reader should be in doubt how your story question will be resolved. (Even though the ultimate outcome is rarely in doubt.)

eg. Though we strongly suspect Katniss will survive against insurmountable odds, she faces huge obstacles in the fight for survival.

So if want to write a great story?

   -Create a compelling story question.

   -Create a character reader's will root for.

   -And a reason why they'll support that character through to the end.

   -Create obstacles; make it look like that character can't obtain what they want.

   -Try to answer your story question in an unexpected way.

STELLAR SETTINGS: BRINGING YOUR STORY TO LIFE

The crux of any good story is character and emotion. You can set your story in Vegas or Paris or the wilds of Africa but unless your readers care about your characters, and those characters are strongly motivated and believable, setting is irrelevant.

But if used correctly, as an adjunct to your powerfully written story, the setting can bring your book alive.

Is the setting evocative?

How many of you have read a book set in Paris and can visualize the Eiffel Tower, the Place de la Concorde, Montmarte? A Roman book, with the Coliseum, the Spanish Steps? Venice with its charming waterways and gondolas?

Mention a city in the world and anyone will have an instant mental image of what that place looks like. Why stop there? If you can layer in sounds, smells and the 'feel' of a place, you'll really bring your story alive.

That's what I hoped to evoke with *FAKING IT*. Set predominantly in India, I wanted to bring this magical, mystical country alive, so I deliberately took my readers on a journey, from the bustling streets of Mumbai to small town, beachside Arnala.

I also layered the story with sights, sounds, aromas and foods of the locality, a good way to enhance the setting.

Here are some examples:

As we entered the main pavilion, a heady wave of aromas washed over me. Pungent freshly ground spices—cumin, coriander and garam masala—interspersed with tangy lime and succulent mango and petite Lady Finger bananas.

I inhaled and my stomach grumbled. Looked like I'd caught Anjali's ravenous disease.

Demonstrating an uncanny ability to read food thoughts, Anjali tugged my arm. "This way. You must try the falooda."

For once she'd get no protest from me. I barely had time to glance at the hundreds of stalls piled high with fresh fruit and vegetables, cheeses and chocolates, plastic flowers, electrical appliances, kitchenware, crockery, and every knick-knack known to man before we stopped at a stall and she ordered the sweet drink.

"Do they sell clothes here?"

She looked me up and down. "Not the kind you'd wear. We'll head to Fashion Street and a few malls later."

Unsure whether she'd insulted or praised me, I accepted my soda fountain glass and gratefully drank. The smooth rosewater-flavored milk, tapioca balls, and rose jelly slid over my tastebuds. Delicious.

Using the taste and smell of food particular to Crawford market in Mumbai enhances this scene. Packs more punch than: "Hungry, Anjali stopped at Crawford Market, bought her usual favorite falooda and we continued on our way."

Here's another example, a snapshot of Mumbai in three concise, evocative sentences:

Fresh flowers on street corners, roadside vendors frying snacks in giant woks, long orderly lines at bus stops. Bustling markets and sprawling malls nestled between ancient monuments.

Amazing contrasts—boutiques and five-star restaurants alongside abject poverty, beggars sharing the sidewalks with immaculately coiffed women who belonged on the cover of Elle, smog-filled streets while the Arabian Sea stretched as far as the eye could see on the city's doorstep.

Another example of concise setting that can convey local flavor:

I woke to the sounds of the Punjabi sweet shop owner abusing a customer in rapid Hindi, a squawking rooster losing a fight with a rabid dog, and Anjali berating Buddy for missing a spot while polishing the car. Gotta love Mumbai mornings.

Weaving a local festival, using description of the event, the colors, etc.... brings this scene alive.

Fake Roman columns surrounded a covered walkway leading to a gazebo, where a harem of women wearing butter-cup, amaranth, and lilac saris spilled down the steps in riotous abandon.

They clapped and twirled and cast coy glances at the male chorus, resplendent in burgundy turbans. My head spun with the noise and color and sheer numbers of extras involved.

Watching a scene shot live would change the way I viewed Bollywood films forever, the vibrancy and animation astounding. The fantastic blur of color and music mesmerized me, as I tapped my foot in time with the catchy tabla rhythm, wishing I could demonstrate the same joie de vivre of the actors. I was particularly impressed with the stunning sari-clad women dancing chakkars (pirouettes) and dhak dhaks (a dance step involving loads of titillating breast jerks), their grace and liveliness inspiring.

Apparently, most male movie fans loved the dhak dhak. Not surprising, considering onscreen kisses were rare, and nudity non-existent, so the odd breast shimmy—often in the rain for a little extra attention—was about as raunchy as it got. Movie audiences would have a group coronary if Stanley Kubrick produced here.

As the music picked up tempo and the dancers whirled in compelling color, I didn't know where to look first, like a kid on a trip to Disneyland.

"You'll like this, child. Holi is the Hindu festival of color and often used in film sequences. Look." Anjali grabbed my arm in excitement and I followed her line of vision.

"Wow." I stared as a cast of hundreds threw bright powders and sprayed water on one another, dancing and singing and leaping in an astonishing kaleidoscope of color. Peacock blue mingled with emerald, ruby with sunshine yellow, a gorgeous mayhem free-for-all like a bunch of hyperactive pre-schoolers let loose with finger-paints. I yearned to play.

Conveying setting is all about the reader 'being in the moment.' Using the right descriptions, somewhere as everyday as a café can be brought to life.

Here's another example from FAKING IT, when Shari's back in NYC:

I sipped at my chai and snuggled into an oversized armchair nearest to the cake counter, people-watching. Students with their book-laden arms and bright-eyed enthusiasm, frazzled moms downing giant cappuccinos in record time while repeatedly glancing at their watches and talking in too-loud voices about lack of sleep and diaper brands, and businessmen sneaking away from the office, hiding behind newspapers, trying to look important but spoiling the effect by reading the funnies rather than the financial news.

Through this melting pot of New York Starbucks culture strode Drew, looking ten times better than I remembered.

Seeing Starbucks through Shari's eyes, seeing the commonalities to any café, will have readers identifying with the setting.

Is first-hand research essential?

I set the bulk of my novels in Melbourne, which makes for easy first-hand research. No prizes for guessing why I've set books in Acland Street (St. Kilda), Lygon St. (Carlton) and the Docklands...food research a must for authenticity!

So did I travel to India? Unfortunately not, but I lived vicariously through relatives. Their firsthand details enabled me to layer details I might've lacked using the Internet alone. And yes, I also spent countless hours on the Net.

If you've chosen a setting you've never visited, it pays to put in a little extra groundwork.

Contact people who live in the area to gather details and give your setting authenticity. People who live in an area can give you specifics, such as weather in a certain month, names of local newspapers, local slang.

Ask friends/family for referrals to local people from that country/city. Talking to people from an area can help bring it alive. My dad was partially raised in Mumbai and hearing his food stories helped me layer that richness in my story.

Read reference books written by people living in the area. Look for sensory details, local language to describe events and places.

The Internet is every author's friend when it comes to research. But a word of warning: sites can be inaccurate, so choose wisely. Blogs from locals living in an area can be particularly useful. Web cams are also useful for seeing what an area looks like: weather, traffic, cars people drive, etc....

Tourist information bureaus are a wealth of local knowledge, and are particularly good for adding local flavor (e.g. things to do, yearly festivities, etc....)

Is it okay to use your imagination?

Writers invent settings all the time. World building of a place, imagined or otherwise, can suck a reader into a book and make them crave the sequel.

Sadly, I've never been on a private jet, but here's what it looked like in my imagination (taken from NOT THE MARRYING KIND)

As the jet taxied along the runway, she glanced at her surroundings, impressed despite her snit with its owner.

Butter-soft leather recliners the color of ripe wheat lined one side of the jet, directly opposite a mahogany bar with forest green leather bar stools edging it. The flat-screen TV above the bar was larger than her bedroom back home. Squishy ochre cushions placed strategically on the chairs highlighted their pristine lushness, while the mahogany coffee tables were so highly polished she could have used them as mirrors.

The opulent luxury made her feel like she'd stumbled into a princess' dream. And that was before she'd been personally served a late lunch of sesame-crusted tempura shrimp served with a watercress and pear salad, rose-stewed figs and baklava, and hand-squeezed lemonade by a steward.

If you've invented a setting, using your imagination to layer in details of smell, taste, feel, can only enhance the picture you're painting for your reader.

Here's an example of Love, a small kitschy town in California that is the setting for my Looking for Love series. This snippet is taken from CRAZY LOVE:

Sierra inhaled as she stepped out into the sunshine, calmed by the sweet, heavy scent of freesias in the air. She loved the delicate pink and white flowers tinged with gold, their heady perfume a reminder of the first time she'd set foot in town and been captivated by the abundance of bright flowers in pots along Main Street.

With Dolores hanging onto her hand for fear she'd bolt she'd been dragged up this street, sullen and silent while her mom grinned at everyone like a newly crowned Miss California greeting fans.

While mom had done the royal wave, Sierra had avoided eye contact and counted pots outside the shop-fronts, focusing on the thin stems and delicate petals to curb the rising panic with every step into town.

She'd lost her dad, her hometown, her school, and her friends in the space of a week. Arriving in Love sucked.

Fear had numbed her feet, anesthetized her heart and produced a healthy distrust of males that lingered to this day but Love had grown on her, had become a comfortable fit and every season the freesias bloomed she was reminded how far she'd come from that scared, lost little girl.

She loved Main Street, its eclectic shops a draw for tourists and locals alike. She regularly shopped at the organic grocer, the toffee store and the coffee house, partial to the freshly ground beans from around the world.

Tourists preferred the funky fashions in a string of tiny boutiques stocking everything from kaftans to love beads, loitered in the aromatherapist's and spent a squillion on souvenirs in Amor's Corner Shop.

The town hadn't lost its cozy charm despite the constant influx of rubberneckers and while there were regular complaints about the lack of restaurants and bars, she liked knowing everyone when she headed to Venus for a Margarita or a delish meal at the Love Shack.

She reached the end of the block, turned left past the grade and high schools, crossed the town square and passed the town hall, following her nose and the scent of soul-reviving coffee as she pushed aside a curtain of hanging beads and stepped into Aphrodite, the best café this side of LA.

While the faded linoleum floor, mismatched tables, wobbly chairs and gingham curtains weren't as aesthetically pleasing as a shiny new Starbucks or Gloria Jeans, the coffees were to die for.

Is accuracy important?

If your setting is front and center (e.g. historicals), how you portray a setting is crucial. Nothing yanks a reader out of a story more than an incongruous detail that doesn't fit a specific time period. So check historical timelines, fashions, foods, whether a building existed or an event happened, topography of the land, etc....to ensure authenticity.

I printed out a Vegas map for this scene from NOT THE MARRYING KIND.

The Strip teemed with life. Goggle-eyed tourists rubbernecking, young guys cruising, local casino employees hurrying to work.

He loved the desert but there was something about this city that made his blood fizz.

He stepped onto the pavement and inhaled, car fumes and designer perfume and dust clogging his nostrils. People jostled him and the bright lights cast a permanent dawn in the sky. Rap music from a passing limo clashed with car horns and the blend of foreign accents from all around.

Yeah, the cosmopolitan buzz had him hooked. He'd traveled extensively for business but whenever he glimpsed the Grand Canyon out of the plane window, he knew he was almost home.

A home that was doing a damn fine job of hiding his wife.

He edged through the crowd, striding through the gaps, scanning ahead. Luckily he only hired the best, and his concierge had pointed which way she'd gone.

The Blackwood, nestled between the Monte Carlo and the Mandarin, was in the heart of prime Strip hotels. Unable to stop a habit of a lifetime, something he'd developed as a young kid the first time his folks brought him here, he mentally recited hotel names.

Aria and Vdara on his left before he hit Harmon, Paris, and Bally's on his right after it.

Memorizing and reciting names had been fun as a kid. Now it served to annoy the hell out of him, as every hotel he passed made him wonder if Poppy had gone into any of them and given him the slip. His heart sank as he passed the Cosmopolitan and Bellagio on his left, crossed Flamingo Ave, and hit Caesar's Palace.

She couldn't have got this far so fast, not in those sky-

high heels. Before he belatedly realized she'd taken them off
before she left.

Dammit, he'd lost her.

Failure didn't sit well with him, never had, and he
clenched his fists, wishing he could punch something.

That was when he caught sight of her, way ahead,
halfway between Mirage and Treasure Island. She was
moving fast, practically jogging, and he broke into a sprint.

Something else I do when scene setting is base a fictional
town/city on a real place. That way, readers who've been to
that town won't pick you up for inconsistencies. eg. There's
no bank on that street corner or the Main Street doesn't
have two hotels on it.

I love choosing settings for my books. The perfect
setting adds richness to the story, a backdrop for your
strongly motivated characters to strut their stuff.

Check facts.

Be inventive.

Most of all, have fun creating your vibrant setting.

METHODOLOGY

Writing processes intrigue me.

How writers write.

Do they plot? Fly by the seat of their pants? Write to music? Write in silence? Have some magical trick to make words pour out?

If a writer's most commonly asked question is 'where do you get your ideas from?' a close second would be 'how do you write your books?'

When I first started writing, I was a plotter.

I played around with character charts, answering questions for my hero and heroine, filling in an art sheet with a basic story outline. It helped me, knowing where I was heading with a story.

Then somewhere along the line I changed.

Completely.

These days, I'm a pantser.

I still do a little pre-writing plotting. I need to know my characters but I focus more on their motivations and what drives them rather than knowing their hobbies and family. I need to know they will be in conflict and how, not their favorite car or their star sign.

So I jot down a page or two of motivations and conflict. And off I go. Flying by the seat of my pants. And the ride is exhilarating.

That said, I'm still intrigued by plotting.

And if I get stuck in the sagging middle or need clarification, I always resort to trusty pen and paper to roughly plot the rest of the story, jotting one-sentence snippets to describe what needs to happen in each chapter to the end of the book.

There's something comforting in having those sentences, like signposts guiding me to the end. And it makes me write quicker too.

I like the uncertainty of not knowing where my characters will lead me.

I like giving them free rein.

But I swear my inner plotter is still tempted by structure, especially lining up color-coded index cards on a wall...

If you love being highly organised, I recommend the writing software Scrivener. I've written my last 40 novels on it and I swear it helps me to write faster. I love color-coding my chapters according to the hero or heroine point of view. I love their character sketch templates. Their index cards. Their word counter. I'm a fan! And the best part? You can trial it free for 30 days. Not 30 consecutive days either, but 30 days total every time you use it.

The software does so much more than what I use it for but I'm rapt using it for the basics.

My advice? Play around with various methods. See what works best for you. Let your creativity dictate how you write a story.

SPEED WRITING

For some of us writing comes as naturally as breathing. It's not who we are but it's something we have to do.

That said, it can be hard work getting those words to make sense, getting those characters to behave and most importantly, getting the lot to make sense in a well-rounded, well-motivated plot that will keep readers turning the pages.

I'm lucky. I'm a fast writer. When I plant my butt in my office chair or on the sofa, I can usually write 3000 words in 2 hours. Some people write more, some people write less and we've all had those days and those books where writing one page is a momentous achievement and we reach for the chocolate as a fitting reward (that's my excuse and I'm sticking to it!)

So is there any magical formula to write faster? I wish. However, here are a few tips that work for me.

1. DON'T EDIT

I usually write 5 days a week from 9.30am-2.00pm, with an hour lunch break usually involving a quick catch up on the latest Netflix show I'm binge watching. I spend the first half hour reading emails, doing promotion, catching up on publishing news and then I focus on the business of writing.

I used to love reading back over the last few pages before I started a day's work but I don't have that luxury anymore. If I have a few hours to write, I want to spend every second of that time writing and that means switching off the internal editor.

I may read the last paragraph I wrote the day before but that's it. Do NOT be tempted to read back any more than that for you will find yourself polishing/editing/rewriting before you know it. And you'll have plenty of time for that later once you've finished the first draft.

2. SET ASIDE W.T.O.

To increase writing speed you need to specifically set aside 'writing time only.' Even if this is ten minutes a day, nothing else happens during that time. Nothing.

No answering phones, no kiddie distractions, nada. If this means you have your W.T.O. late at night or early in the morning before family life takes over, so be it. Yes, you'll be tired. Yes, you could use those extra hours of sleep but just think of all those words adding up into a nice, juicy manuscript much faster than you dreamed possible.

3. IGNORE THE INTERNET

The ultimate distraction...it's so easy to research/network/promote/play on the Internet. We all need the Net. We'd all be lost without it but if you want to increase your writing speed, set aside a time frame when you ignore the Net completely. Even if you're expecting an email from your editor/agent/publisher (okay, you can be a little lax here and keep your inbox open but do NOT check it every time you hear a beep.)

4. PERFECTION? WHAT'S THAT?

I'm a bit of a perfectionist. I like my first draft to not need a lot of editing at the end. I used to be so bad that I'd need the perfect word in a particular scene before I could move on. Not good. This is a classic time waster.

These days if the word doesn't come to me instantly I highlight and move on. Much quicker and it doesn't disrupt thought processes half as much. The best part? When you go back to polish, it's amazing how many times that word you couldn't think of before pops out of nowhere and is a perfect fit.

5. SKIPPING IS GOOD

No, not the rope variety (exercising is not my thing.) Why not skip a scene? Skip a chapter? Skip the whole sagging middle and jump straight to the conclusion?

If a scene/chapter/etc. isn't working for you, don't get bogged down staring at a blank page. Skip ahead.

Write a totally unrelated scene but one that's so clear in your head that the words fly from your fingertips and you can't type fast enough.

The conclusion clear in your head? Write it.

Remember, time is precious and you want to make the most of every minute so why get bogged down in a scene that isn't working when you could be letting those words flow?

6. GET IN TRAINING

The more you write, the faster you will become.

If you can't write every day (and let's face it, we all need time out which is why I have weekends off) try to write as often as possible. Whether it be short blocks throughout the day or a few times a week, get into the habit of writing.

Train yourself to sit at the computer for W.T.O.

Practice all the hints above but most of all, make writing a ritual.

Trust me, the more you do it, the easier it becomes (well, that's the theory anyway.)

After 80 books, I can say I write faster now than I did at the start. It's a routine for me. I've trained for it. The more you write, the faster you will become.

7. SIZE DOES MATTER

At times portability is the key to speed. I love writing on my MacAir. For some reason, being able to write on the sofa/in a cafe/in the car, helps me write faster.

In the past, I used Alphie. Alphasmart is a portable word processor which runs on 3 AA batteries, can sit on your lap quite comfortably and can slip into the average handbag.

But the best part? Alphie turns you into a speed machine because you can't edit. You can't compulsively check page count by glancing at the top right hand corner of the screen every few pages. You can't do much of anything but sit there and let the words flow.

When I'm stuck or bogged down or just need a change of pace I grab Alphie, plop on the sofa and write. Usually for an hour non-stop (the keys are quite clunky so I get a bit tired of it after that). It's amazing how many words you get when you upload onto your PC the next day.

So go ahead and fall for Alphie too. I'm happy to share.

That said, because I'm juggling several publishers at the moment and need access to the Internet, I tend to write on a laptop these days. I still get the portability factor but I can answer editors at a moment's notice if I need to.

8. SPRINTING

Anything above walking pace is too fast for me, so I'm not talking about sprints of the running variety. These days, the only sprinting I do is in relation to writing.

Basically, it involves writing as fast as you can in a certain time frame, non-stop. No interruptions, no distractions, just fingers flying across the keyboard.

I once heard Stephanie Bond recommend using an egg timer to pace yourself but these days many authors join forces in small groups on Twitter to ramp up the speed.

#1K1hr is a well-known hash tag. Writing one thousand words in one hour. Anyone can join in. Just put the call out on Twitter and you're bound to have several writers to join you in sprint madness.

And that's another thing. Sprinting in a group tends to up the ante. For me, it brings out my competitiveness and I try to write as fast as I can.

Sprints work particularly well for me when I have a short deadline and loads of words to write. Maybe it's the added pressure? Maybe it's knowing I have to report back my word count to fellow writers after the spring? Whatever it is, I write faster when I sprint. And I sprint anywhere: early morning, at school pick-up, late at night.

When I sprint, I can write anywhere between 10000 to 20000 words in a week.

Usually, I aim for 8 pages in a day. When I sprint, I can write 8 pages in an hour.

Along with faster fingers, I think your mind loosens, gets in tune with your story, knowing you need to pour the words out to meet your self-imposed time limit.

Practice your sprinting.

You'll be pleased with the results.

My final piece of advice? Remember, speed isn't everything. Ultimately, it's about getting those words to jump from our imaginations onto the page and creating a great story. So do whatever works for you.

Writing is magical, exhilarating and hard work. If we can do it that little bit faster, great. If not, remember the tortoise and the hare!

THE POWER OF ONE SYLLABLE

After almost two decades in publishing, with 80 books published and over 8 million copies sold worldwide, you'd think I'd know what I'm doing, right?

Wrong.

The publishing world changes faster than my kids' favourite TV shows. Just when I think I have a grip on it, something comes along to scuttle my carefully laid plans. Plans that evolved something like this:

2004-first book released with Harlequin Mills & Boon. Plan to write 100 books for them.

2011-sell to a new publisher before they open their doors because of attractive royalty rate of 40% cover price. Make a killing with one book, so-so sales with others.

2012-release first indie title to test the waters. Blown away by sales and earnings.

2013-decide to be a hybrid author. Release more indie titles while juggling traditional contract commitments. Branch into other genres like young adult, release 2 titles with 2 different publishers.

2014- the year I learned the power of that one little syllable. NO. Because maintaining a manic writing pace for a decade, producing 4 category romances and a mainstream novel a year (along with the accompanying revisions, edits, promo, etc...) eventually catches up with you.

NO is the most powerful word a writer will ever learn/write/utter.

Because if you're anything like me—the old me—you never said no.

Your editor, who you adore, asks you to write an online story between books? Sure.

She wants you to be part of an exciting continuity? No probs, sign me up.

She wants you to write for another series in addition to your first? No worries.

Join group blogs and judge competitions and be prolific on social media? Absolutely.

Be interviewed by countless media outlets to help launch a new branch of an established company? Hell yeah.

See a pattern here? I was the ultimate 'yes-girl'. Taking on too much, thriving under pressure, while raising two young kids and managing my hubby's business.

Then 2014 happened and my body made me say NO.

No to a sparkly three book contract from one of the Big 5.

No to continuing a YA series I love.

No to contracts that may look okay on paper but ultimately wouldn't earn me more than the advance.

No to writing for a different series.

No to the many loops I'd been on (unsubscribing isn't a crime!)

No to the constant sharing on Twitter (you may see me on there once a day now.)

Because ultimately, publishing for me is a job. I need a good income to support my family. And in my previous life as a physiotherapist, no way would I say yes to every single thing I was asked to do. So why was I compelled to say yes for the past ten years while writing?

Fear.

Writers are driven by fear. We fear the blank page/the first review/the second book blues/poor sales/bad critiques/losing contracts...I could go on.

I feared not having a contract.

A common fear among many unpublished writers.

We're often so desperate to sign that first-or tenth, or twentieth-contract that we overlook major red flags. Don't do this. It's okay to say NO.

For me, learning to say no took time but once I embraced that syllable, I felt liberated. The pressure lifted and I'm still productive and motivated without the extraneous constraints weighing me down.

Saying NO has been my savior.

Publishing will continue to evolve. The writing community will grow. Books will flood the market, whether traditionally or indie.

And it's great to know that among all this excitement/chaos, we hold the power to manage our careers with that one little syllable...

CREATING HOT HEROES: ALPHA V BETA

Great characters draw me into a story and make me reluctant to put a book down. And nothing signals 'page turner' more than a hot hero.

We all know the type of guy: strong yet gentle, commanding yet compassionate, in control but willing to bend to the heroine's will. Throw in gorgeous with a sense of humor and you've got me well and truly hooked.

So how do you create hot heroes in your writing?

Is your hero a take-control alpha guy or a laid-back beta?

Every hero is different and having an alpha hero in a contemporary romance will be different to an alpha guy in a thriller.

Here are a few points to help you delineate between the two.

• Make him commanding: the alpha hero is always in control. He likes to call the shots - except when the heroine finally tames him.

• Arrogant? Maybe just a tad...the alpha believes in himself and the reach of his influence. Until the battle with his feelings for the heroine begins.

• Passionate: sensual and sexy, the alpha uses his charm and power to get what he wants, though his need for the heroine may ultimately prove stronger.

• Status: impossibly wealthy, probably self-made; the alpha often has celebrity status in the media. The ruler of all he surveys, be it a company or a country. Perhaps a specialist in his field?

• Tower of Strength: the alpha has a steely core, is not easily manipulated and is uncompromising about the things that matter.

• Aspirational: an alpha hero is the guy with whom women aspire to spend the rest of their lives, definitely Mr. Right.

• Code of Honor: the alpha has a strong sense of right and wrong, is reasonable and fair.

• Sense of Humor: the beta hero can laugh at himself and life.

• Follower: Betas are more followers where alphas are leaders.

• Self-Aware: Betas have more insight when it comes to what's going on and how they're feeling.

• Easy going: Betas are the laid-back hero whereas alphas are more driven.

• Outgoing: Betas are more sociable where alphas are more reserved.

• Insecure: Betas may have self-doubts whereas alphas are secure in themselves and their place in the world. Alphas are confident, betas less so.

• Verbal: Betas aren't afraid to express themselves whereas alphas tend to be less verbal and more into the short command, used to having their orders obeyed.

• The 'Nice' Guy: Betas are perceived as 'nice' or 'funny'

or even 'geeky' whereas alphas are perceived as aloof or unobtainable, even the bad boy.

Keep all these in mind when creating your very own hot hero but remember, your hero will be unique. He may demonstrate more of these characteristics than others. He may turn out to be more beta than alpha or vice versa.

And where does the gamma hero fit into all this? Gamma is a combination of alpha and beta, which would make him the perfect man. A tad too perfect for a written hero, perhaps?

Whatever you do, make your man the sexiest hero possible, the kind of guy we can't close the pages on until the last, satisfying scene.

RACIALLY DIVERSE CHARACTERS

The biggest thing authors should be mindful of when writing racially diverse characters is to avoid clichés. Nothing jars a reader out of story more than a cringe-worthy cliché. Like with creating any characters, keep it real. Strong, believable motivations are key. Without the need for a liberal peppering of accents, head-nods, exotic eyes and dusky features.

In creating racially diverse characters, there are so many wonderful aspects to consider: the locations, the food, the fashion, the culture, the traditions. Bringing these aspects to life will enrich the story and help your characters to leap off the page, without the need for cliches.

Here are a few examples from **FAKING IT**:

LOCATION: *I squeezed my eyes shut for the hundredth time as a small child darted out after a mangy dog right in front of our car. On the upside, every time I reopened my eyes, something new captured my attention. Fresh flowers on street corners, roadside vendors frying snacks in giant woks,* long, orderly lines at bus stops. Bustling markets and sprawling malls nestled between ancient monuments.

Amazing contrasts—boutiques and five-star restaurants alongside abject poverty, beggars sharing the sidewalks with immaculately coiffed women who belonged on the cover of Elle, smog-filled streets while the Arabian Sea stretched as far as the eye could see on the city's doorstep.

FOOD: *I'd never tried the renowned chaat, fast-food. With Anjali dragging me toward the nearest stall, it looked like I was about to.*

She ordered and I watched, fascinated, as the young guy manning the stall dextrously laid out a neat row of papadi (small, crisp fried puris—flatbreads) and filled them with a mix of puffed rice, sev, onions, potatoes, green chilies, and an array of chutneys.

I may not have been hungry but the tantalizing aromas of tamarind, mango, and coriander made my mouth water.

MORE FOOD: *"Aloo gobi, avail, murgh masala, dhansak, and rasam."*

"I'm in heaven." He clutched his stomach as he sat. "Want me to serve you?"

"Please, a little of everything." I sipped at my wine as he dished spicy potato, mixed vegetable curry made from coconut and yogurt, and chicken in a tomato, ginger, and spicy sauce. He added lamb cooked with dahl and a dollop of rice, spooning rasam over the rice. I could get used to being served. Serviced. Whatever.

AND MORE (Food is an important part of Indian culture.) *The aromas hit me first and I inhaled* deeply, the heady mix of cumin and mustard seeds and garam masala making me salivate. Food covered every surface, from the samosa-filled platters on the spotless stainless steel counters to the layered shelves in glass cabinets lining every wall. I didn't know where to look first: the tiffin snacks, the street vendor food, or the sweets, arranged in towering pyramids that made my waist as well as my eyes bulge by looking.

CULTURE: As the music picked up tempo and the dancers whirled in compelling color, I didn't know where to look first, like a kid on a trip to Disneyland.

"You'll like this, child. Holi is the Hindu festival of color and often used in film sequences. Look." Anjali grabbed my arm in excitement and I followed her line of vision.

"Wow." I stared as a cast of hundreds threw bright powders and sprayed water on one another, dancing and singing and leaping in an astonishing kaleidoscope of color. Peacock blue mingled with emerald, ruby with sunshine yellow, a gorgeous mayhem free-for-all like a bunch of hyperactive preschoolers let loose with finger paints. I yearned to play.

FASHION: I'd never been to a Hindu wedding, and the traditions enthralled me: Rita and Rakesh tied together by their scarves and walking seven times around a fire, Rakesh placing a black and gold necklace around Rita's neck and putting red powder in her hair parting. Intriguing stuff.

I would've enjoyed it more if I'd understood a word of what the priest said, but the hour-long ceremony was conducted in Sanskrit. The enchanting, important mantras went straight over my head. The bride and groom radiated a happy glow; no translation necessary.

Rakesh made a maroon kurta, the guy's version of a salwaar kameez, hot, though the top ended mid-calf and made him look like an elegant Aladdin. After the ceremony Rita changed into a stunning red sharara for the reception, a sexy salwaar kameez edged in gold jeri like her sari.

In each of these snippets, I've brought the diverse characters to life by utilizing the senses and observations. Immerse your reader in a culture. Help them visualize being in the unique setting you've created. Let them feel the culture.

Anything is achievable with research. I had to do a lot of research to write FAKING IT. And I mean a lot. Countless hours interviewing Indian friends and reading non-fiction books and scouring the Internet for facts. It's a big ask and I think it would be easier to write a protagonist from a particular racial background if the writer shared that background too.

As for cringe-worthy generalisations, it's all in the execution. If the taxi driver in a story absolutely has to be Indian to further the plot, or it's an intrinsic part of the plot, then that's okay, otherwise it's a cliché. And as writers, we want to hold a reader's attention because of the beauty of our prose and the pure escapism of our plot. Don't give them a reason to mark the book as a dreaded DNF.

DEFYING DOUBT DEMONS

Ever had the feeling you're a one-book wonder? Written the dream book only to be paralyzed by fear you won't come up with another plot? Had words fly from your fingertips for one story only to find you sit at the computer for the next and nada? Submitted to a barrage of agents, convinced they'll all hate your work? Entered a competition then wished you hadn't? Delivered your next book to your editor, sure it's the worst drivel ever?

If you answered yes to any of the above, chances are you've had doubt demons perched on your shoulder, whispering nasty insinuations in your ear and generally making an annoying nuisance of themselves.

Doubts plague us all. From New York Times best sellers to newbies flush from their first sale, doubts can hound us, stifling our creativity, making us feel frauds or at their worst, causing writer's block.

Doubts that plague us the most

I love the rush of starting a new book. The thrill of getting a new idea out there, the buzz of two characters strutting onto a page and doing their thing. However, after writing 70 books, the same doubt niggles every time I sit down to start. "Can I do this again?"

I stare in disbelief at the books I've written lined up on my shelf. I pick one up, flip open the cover, flick through the pages, blown away I created that story. And wondering how I'm going to do it again.

It's the same every book yet once I get that opening sentence on the page, I'm off. Demons begone. And it looks like I'm not alone.

Linda Ford (Harlequin Love Inspired Historicals) says, "I have two major doubts that plague me. The first is that I have nothing of importance to say in my stories. I don't write anything (my doubts say) of true significance like those other authors who write such powerful stories of love, forgiveness, healing, etc. etc. My other major doubt is that my writing is immature. My doubts take on an internal voice and carry on a tirade like this: "Not another 'her heart leaped'. Can't you come up with anything just a little less clichéd? Just a little, is all I ask. How hard can it be? If you say sigh one more time I'm going to scream. Etc...."

The fear of repetition is a common one, especially among multi-published authors. Can I make each book fresh? Put a new twist on a tried and true theme? Avoid repeating favorite words? Individualize my characters and not have my thirtieth hero sounding like my second?

For some writers, like Jenna Kernan (Harlequin Historicals) the doubts are more personal. "All your mistakes are now in print for everyone to see and they will never go away. Complete strangers will read and judge my book. Oh, my God, my boss will read those steamy love scenes. Everyone has a person that they dread seeing their work, whose opinion you value or whose censure you fear.

Topping my list are my mother, boss and male co-workers. I worry if I have exposed too much of myself. Have I betrayed family secrets that might embarrass loved ones or friends?"

Jackie Braun (Harlequin Romance) reminds us how our personal life can fuel doubts. "The biggest doubt I've ever run into-and boy did it affect my writing-occurred just after my dad's death in January 2006. I simply lost the joy I'd had in writing. I wondered why I was doing it, if it mattered. I couldn't seem to get into my characters. I wasn't excited about what was happening between them or where it was heading. I was completely numb. This lasted for nearly three books. I described it to friends as trying to run through molasses. Finishing those books was an exhausting process and far from satisfying. Honestly, I don't know how I got through it. I just took it one day and one page at a time. Eventually, the fog and doubts lifted. Little by little the joy has been returning. All I can say is, what a relief."

Other doubts expressed include:

- **Can I write another story people will want to read?**
- **Have I peaked with this book?**
- **Is this book as good as it can be?**
- **Can I write another full story?**
- **I'm great at starting new stories but can I finish this book?**
- **My characters suck. If I don't like them, how can I expect readers to?**
- **Will I meet my deadline?**
- **Will my editor like my revisions?**
- **Will the book sell and make money?**
- **Will the reviewers and readers hate it?**

- **Will the publisher regret giving me a chance?**

By far the most common doubt expressed by authors is 'will this book be as good as the last?'

As writers, it looks like doubts prevail, in varying degrees, for us all.

Have doubts affected your writing?

Tracy Montoya (Harlequin Intrigue) says "On a bad day, I'll just stop writing altogether. But on a good day, I use those worries to make myself a better writer. If I'm worried about being cliché or purple, I'll go back over what I've already written and really take a close look at everything, revising until its better."

While doubts can affect our writing, the added pressures that come with being published can exacerbate them. Meeting deadlines, revisions, copy edits, promotion, maintaining a website, cover art questions, newsletter mailings all serve to increase our doubts. Once published, you've made a serious commitment. What if you can't meet the demands? Great, yet another doubt!

"We all get stuck. We either try to follow rules that don't work for us, and ignore rules that do; or we find ourselves writing the same books over and over for fear of losing our readers if we do something a little different. We wonder if we'll ever receive recognition for our unique talent. It's easy to say bad reviews don't matter, but the criticism stings. It's easy to write that rejection is part of the business, but every rejection has us wondering if maybe we're pursuing the wrong dream." Allison Brennan (NYT Bestseller) makes a great point here, in that following rules and guidelines are often used to get a grip on our doubts and try to wrestle them into some semblance of control. But what if those rules only serve to constrict us further? What then? How do we banish these doubts?

Methods used to banish doubts

Jacqueline Diamond (Harlequin American Romance) has written over eighty novels spanning a twenty-five year career, and has valuable insight for us. "How do I combat doubts? Simply by the love of writing. As my latest story and characters come to life, plot twists pop into my mind along with insights and funny lines. They remind me that my gifts don't depend on whether an editor or agent appreciates them -- although of course I'm eager for that, as well. Exterior validation is wonderful. But the joy of creating my books belongs exclusively to me, and I hope I never lose that."

Bonnie Vanak (Harlequin Nocturne) says that the trick is to beat the demons into submission and not let them take over to the point of crippling your writing. "When I go through a period of doubting my writing, I have friends who are very supportive and they reassure me it's the DDD syndrome (Dreaded Doubt Demon). I have a sign on my wall from a good author friend, Norah Wilson, who emailed me words of wisdom once. It reads "Trust and have faith in your own writing and if that fails, borrow someone else's faith in your writing." When you think of the story, and find an element that drives you to tell the story, be it a character, a plot point, the setting or conflict and motivation, and you find the excitement that compelled you to begin writing, those doubt demons often fade away into the background."

For some, like Dana Marton (Harlequin Intrigue) resorting to trusty pen and paper and making concrete lists can help. "Once I realized just how much power I have given my doubts, I came up with a little exercise to take that power back. Anyone can do this. Take a blank sheet of paper and draw a line down the middle. On the left, list your doubts. When you are done, on the right turn each of these doubts into a huge positive. The left side could be called "Why I think I won't succeed." And the right side could be called "How I know I will succeed." As an example, one of mine at the top of the list was: I don't have an English degree. My writing is probably terrible. Editors would faint at the sight of my grammatical mistakes. I counteracted this with: I have degrees in other subjects that make my writing authentic when I incorporate those subjects into my books. I have a varied background that includes several industries and global experiences, which will add interest to my books. These will more than make up for any grammatical errors. Publishers have editors in the first place so they can catch errors. Writers without any kind of formal training, without a college degree or a high school degree even, had made it to the bestseller lists, received major prizes and awards. And so can I! I had a long list of doubts that I put to paper in detail then took the time to neutralize/turn into a positive."

For other writers, it's all about trust. "Even when I feel as if what I'm writing doesn't hold together, just keep going. Eventually I'll get to a better spot, and most importantly, I can improve it during the rewriting. What I usually find is that my first instincts are right. When I reread, it's not as bad as I thought. There's even a lot of good stuff!" says Ruth Axtell Morren (A Man Most Worthy)

Some writers rely on friends. "I enlist the help of my critique partner who kicks my butt. One of her trademark lines is, "You can do this." And sometimes it becomes about making it fun again, so I'll have a brainstorm session with friends." Donna Alward (Harlequin American/St. Martin's Press.)

Double RITA finalist Anna Campbell (Seven Nights in a Rogue's Bed) takes the 'Bird by Bird' approach. "Just do the next word, the next sentence, the next paragraph. Don't look at the scary big picture."

For me, it's about facing down that blank page. I shut those little doubt critters up by getting words down on a page. I give myself permission to write whatever comes into my head, I type fast, I switch off my internal editor and don't obsess about individual words. I don't re-read as I'm going, I just write. It's amazing what seeing those words pile up can do for my confidence. And remember, you can edit and revise words; you can't do that to a blank page.

DREAMING

I get many of my ideas/titles/first lines/characters in that half drowsy/half awake state just before dropping off to sleep.

In fact, if I need to ponder a plot point or a conflict that isn't quite working, I'll go to bed, close my eyes and let my mind wander.

It's a great technique and often works. (Drifting off to nap is a bonus!)

Imagine my surprise when I discovered there's a technical term for this.

There is a naturally occurring sleep state called the HYPNAGOGIC STATE.

As I've already described, it is the phase of sleep before you drift off and before you wake up, and is a state of altered consciousness.

Apparently it's a highly fertile time for creative people.

The trick is to utilize this phase.

Ask yourself a question before you lie down.

e.g. What is the main obstacle keeping my characters apart?

Close your eyes.

Let your mind drift…doze…

But you must remember what happens in this state.

I've heard a recommendation to hold one arm up in the air, as the tension required holding the arm up will keep you on the verge of that sleep/awake state, and as the ideas/concepts/connections come, you immediately write them down.

For me, I close my eyes, let the ideas flow, and jot them as soon as they arrive.

It's a tried and trusty plotting method for me.

As a follow on from this, let's discuss dream journals.

Personally, I've never had a dream that has resulted in a book, though I've heard some authors have.

For me, it's that pre-dream state which is a cauldron of bubbling ideas.

Our subconscious never sleeps so why not tap into it?

The art of keeping a dream journal is simple.

Keep a notebook and pen by the bed.

The instant you wake (whether it be morning or middle of the night), don't move. Stay still and relaxed, try to remember your dreams or anything else you can think of.

Initially you may only get vague details. A rose. The color purple. Kids running.

Or perhaps a pervading feeling will come through…fear, happiness…

Whatever you barely remember, write it down.

Start to court your dreams. The more committed you are, the more vivid your dreams may become.

Trying new ways to harness creative energy is fun. Why not give it a try?

SAMPLE SYNOPSES

The bane of any writer's existence is writing a synopsis.

For pantsers like me, who have no idea what will happen in the story until I write it...well, let's just say it's a form of torture.

And even for plotters, who like to know plot points before they write a story, having to outline the entire book in succinct paragraphs can be a challenge.

Here, I've shown two methods I use.

The first, for CRAZY LOVE, is the traditional version.

The second, for NOT THE MARRYING KIND, is a method I've tinkered with over the years and it's the one I use all the time now.

I find it gives me clarity to do brief outlines of hero, heroine, storyline, conflicts and motivation. These are the essence of any story and having those few pages done before I start writing a story helps me when I need to refer back later.

Those of you who've read both books will find the synopses particularly interesting, to see how much the books vary or stick closely to the initial outlines.

CRAZY LOVE SYNOPSIS

Sierra Kent doesn't do love.

It's too complicated, too painful and easier to compartmentalise as part of her job rather than confront in her life. While she delights in matchmaking her clients through her Internet dating agency Love Byte, she doesn't trust her intuition when it comes to the one emotion that has repeatedly let her down for as long as she cares to remember.

Being the apple of her daddy's eye wasn't enough to keep him in her life and he abandoned her when she was ten, leading to major upheaval when her heartbroken mum relocated to Love, a few hours south of LA.

While her mum seemed content to drink wheatgrass juice, polish crystals and tie-dye the odd sarong or two, Sierra had to contend with being the new kid on the block, quickly learning that a stinging comeback and sharp wit were necessities for a freckle-faced, red-haired ten year old with a chip on her shoulder because she didn't have a daddy.

And though she initially rebelled against Love and all it stood for, she soon came around thanks to the stabilising influence of Hank Stevens, a recently widowed farmer. As the years passed, Sierra grew to depend on Love and all it represented: permanence, reliability and security, three things she craved as a child and never had. Now, twenty years later, Sierra has a chance to repay Hank. Her dating agency is one of the most prominent in the country and acts as the catalyst in a life-changing reaction for the one man who has never let her down.

Olivia Fairley, recently divorced and looking for love, is perfect for Hank in every way and Sierra is ecstatic when the older couple meets and falls head over heels thanks to her trusty computer. And when Uncle Hank asks her to take on the role of wedding planner, the only favour he has ever requested, she sees it as one small way she can repay him for a lifetime of unswerving love and support. However, her goal to see the happy couple wed hits a snag when Marc Fairley, Olivia's son, bowls into town with the sole intention of putting a stop to the wedding.

City-slick Marc, CEO of A-Corp, one of the LA's premier acquisition corporations, doesn't have time for Love. From the minute he enters the kitschy town he can't wait to hotfoot it back to LA with his deranged mother in tow. After all, she'd have to be to even consider marrying some hick farmer a scant few months after divorcing his father and worse, to spend her life holed up in this backwater place.

Love is every bit as bad as the real thing and he should know: raised by parents who co-existed in frosty silences—an abusive father who drove his mother to alcoholism—and divorced less than a year into his own disastrous marriage many years ago, he knows love is a crock.

Keen to acquire info on Hank before confronting the senile pair, he barges into Love Byte for a showdown with the proprietor, the person who had a major hand in the fiasco. However, rather than squaring up to a charlatan as expected, he's astounded by the sassy redhead who sparks his interest with her quick wit and killer body. Rather than providing him with the low-down on this Hank character his mother is smitten with, Sierra tells him to butt out and in an effort to get the information he wants he agrees to have dinner with the enemy, though he'd much rather be sleeping with her.

When dinner at the local diner extends to coffee at Sierra's place, Marc is none the wiser about his mother's new relationship. Sierra has thwarted him and to his surprise he doesn't mind. He has actually enjoyed sparring with the brash redhead and isn't sure what to expect next. Whatever it

is, it isn't to discover her secret condom stash, her vulnera-
bility to the emotion she touts for a living or her impressive
kissing technique.

Sierra, surprised by Marc's intention to break up the
happy couple, issues a challenge in order to buy some time
for Hank in the hope Marc will grow to like the man given
half a chance. Her challenge is simple: if Marc sticks around
for a week, gets to know Hank and respects his mother's rela-
tionship, she will stall the wedding.

Never one to back down, especially when his adversary
intrigues him on so many levels, Marc stays in Love. Despite
growing to like Hank, Marc's gut instinct tells him the old
man is hiding something. However, he is distracted by his
own business and the biggest dilemma he has ever faced.
Once A-Corp acquires the top 5 US Internet companies and
sells them off, his company will take over the number one
mantle in the country and more importantly, oust his father
from the top spot.

Against her better judgment, Sierra drops her guard and
lets Marc into her life. He's there for her when the father she
resents dies. He charms her without trying and after getting
to know him better and having the best sex of her life, she
acknowledges that he might be 'The One'. What if it is fate,
destiny, that each person has a predestined soul mate and
better yet, what if she's just found him, only to be deprived
when he heads out of her life and back to LA?

Maybe the annual Love Fest is the opportunity she has
been hoping for, a chance to see how committed Marc is to a
future for them. After all, what man can shun love when
bombarded with it in every way, shape and form? However,
before she can test her mum's wacky soul mate theory, Marc
shows his true colours and the first she learns of his treachery
is via the newspapers.

To Marc's surprise, Love Fest draws huge media coverage and before he knows it, reporters descend on him demanding to know why he's in Love. Unable to tell the truth about his plans to sabotage his mother's new relationship, or the scarier truth that he may have succumbed to love, he confirms he's in town on business. In a flash, the media come to the conclusion that Love Byte's prominent position in the IT world and A-Corp's latest coup is linked and with some investigative reporting, lay the story out in the tabloids.

Sierra is devastated to learn the truth. She has taken a chance on love and it has blown up in her face though this time she doubts if she'll ever recover from the detonation. Marc used her and worse, is about to take the only constant in her life, her hard-earned business. She tells him to leave her alone in no uncertain terms and sets about saving Love Byte with Uncle Hank's help.

Forced to choose between A-Corp and revenge on his father or his love for Sierra, Marc realises there is no contest. He heads back to LA to wrap up unfinished business before returning to Love on Christmas Eve for his mum's wedding and to seal the deal of a lifetime, the one involving his heart.

And though Sierra and Marc are aware a union between them will create enough sparks to send Love up in flames, they prove that winning isn't important in the love stakes it's how you play the game.

Compare the CRAZY LOVE synopsis to the proposal for NOT THE MARRYING KIND and you'll see the key differences.

NOT THE MARRYING KIND SYNOPSIS

HEROINE: **Poppy Collins** *would do anything for the sister who raised her, including travel from outer-LA suburbia Provost to Las Vegas in a last ditch stand to keep Vanessa's party planning business afloat. Being summoned by one of the richest men in Nevada to throw is best mate a divorce party is one thing but marrying the guy to save her sister? Crazy!*

HERO: **Beck Blackwood** *has a multi-million dollar deal on the table but his conservative investors are getting angsty. They don't want a renowned playboy as the face of their country-wide campaign so to nail this all-important deal and become the face of high-end construction across America, Beck needs something he never thought he'd want: a wife. And what better woman to agree to a marriage of convenience than a suburban party planner, a confirmed romance cynic with no danger of complicating their expiration-date marriage with emotion?*

STORYLINE:

Poppy Collins will do anything for her sister Vanessa.

Her emotionally absentee parents Ruth and Earl didn't raise her, Vanessa did, picking up the slack left by the two most self-absorbed people on the planet.

Vanessa is her sister and best friend rolled into one, so when Vanessa's marriage falls apart and she plunges into a depression that affects her business, Poppy has no alternative but to step in. It's the least she can do for the years of support Vanessa has given her.

So Poppy the part-time marketing whiz becomes Poppy the party planner, using the expertise she has picked up from Vanessa when helping out occasionally to save Vanessa's business.

With divorce parties becoming all the rage, Poppy insti-gates a campaign to boost business and has a chance to land a highly lucrative account: throwing a major divorce party for a friend of a renowned Vegas playboy.

If she nails this pitch, the party planning business will boom again and the only thing Vanessa has left these days will be saved.

However, Poppy doesn't count on facing off with Beck Blackwood, the notoriously tough businessman with a playboy reputation. Everyone in Nevada has heard of tough-guy-made-good Beck, the construction king with the Midas touch.

But what Poppy doesn't count on is her physical reaction to the sexy bad boy, experiencing a real spark for the first time ever.

When Beck proposes a marriage of convenience at her pitch appointment, she tells him where to stick it. Until he threatens to undermine her and her sister's business and she'd left with no alternative: marry Beck and save Vanessa's business or risk losing everything. Vanessa's mental health is too fragile to toy with so Poppy sucks it up and agrees to marry the playboy, with a clear end-date in mind.

He solidifies his reputation with a good, old-fashioned, small town girl as his wife and pacifies his angsty investors who won't take a chance on a flashy Vegas playboy, she saves her sister's business. Win-win.

However, while Beck needs a conservative wife, Poppy proves to be anything but and he's smitten!

Poppy's first impressions of Beck and his schmoozy, bright-lights, city image are challenged by the surprisingly intimate chapel wedding and his desert house. The playboy isn't all trappings and glitz: he's heat and dry wit and down-

to-earth, with a love for the desert she soon comes to appreciate through his eyes.

As the two give in to their sizzling attraction, grow closer and are forced to unwittingly re-evaluate their emotion/tangle-free arrangement, their respective businesses are heading for a crash.

One of Beck's investors discovers Poppy's anonymous online Divorce Diva Daily business and threatens to derail his entire deal if Poppy doesn't stop perpetuating divorce frivolity (and undermining core marriage values).

Beck has to make a choice: side with his wife, who he has growing feelings for and lose out on his dream of taking his construction business national (and gaining the ultimate vindication) or relentlessly pursue his dream and lose Poppy in the process.

Suddenly, his win-win has turned into lose-lose and he doesn't like it, not one bit.

The situation is worsened when the wife he has fallen for believes he's responsible for leaking her identity, sabotaging her anonymity and undermining everything they've worked so hard for, including their burgeoning relationship.

She sees it as an underhanded way to run, as he's done his entire life, and the resultant fallout from their soul-deep revelations threatens to tear them apart forever.

Can the two relationship cynics meet halfway and believe in their commitment to have the happily ever after they deserve?

CONFLICT/MOTIVATION:
Poppy is driven by her desire for self-preservation.

Poppy sees depending on anyone else for happiness as a sure-fire way to open up for heartache. It happened with her parents (too wrapped up in each to worry about her, letting her down repeatedly from a young age, only to ultimately divorce) and her sister, who adored her husband only to have him leave her after 'falling out of love', and the ensuing devastation on Vanessa and her business.

Poppy sees relationships as flawed and inevitably painful so protects her independence fiercely. Casual dating is fine, anything beyond, no way. Marriage would be her ultimate nightmare therefore instigating divorce parties to celebrate people regaining their freedom is right up her alley! She sees a marriage of convenience to save her sister's business as no threat because it's for money, no feelings involved. Perfect!

Beck is driven by his desire for success.

For Beck, success equals recognition and vindication, which he never had growing up. Raised by his grandfather in the poor end of a small desert town, he hated being shunned for his upbringing and vowed to make good and show the lot of them.

Despite his business success now, having investors doubt him because of his lifestyle harks back to his upbringing when everyone doubted him because of his parental stock, therefore he must do whatever it takes, including marry for convenience, to nail this deal, gain national recognition and prove to everyone he isn't tainted by the deadbeat label of his past.

Poppy is impulsive, rash, flirty and passionate.

Beck is charming, determined, cynical, driven.

Poppy craves independence.

Beck craves recognition.

Poppy learns that trusting a guy doesn't always mean loss of self (as she has seen with her mum and sister.)

Beck learns that relying on someone else for helps isn't

always a bad thing (and that not everyone in his life will let him down.)

SETTING: *Las Vegas*

I know which I prefer: the second proposal is quick, to the point, an outline of the book at a glance.

There are many 'how to' articles on synopsis writing available.

Read a few.

Make notes.

Play around.

Find your niche.

And write the best synopsis you can so an editor or agent is begging to see your book.

STUCK

With the bulk of my books, once I'm heading towards the end scene, the words are tumbling out so fast my fingers can barely keep up.

My characters are aching to get their happily-ever-after. They need resolution.

And I want to tie up all those niggly loose ends I've created throughout the book.

But what happens when I'm stuck?

I remember seeing somewhere in my publishing industry travels that the prolific, mega-successful Nora Roberts doesn't believe in writer's block and I have to say I agree.

Now don't get me wrong. Not all books flow easily for me. I do get stuck occasionally. Life intervenes.

When I lost my grandmother, who was my biggest fan, I couldn't write anything for months. Ever had that feeling right before an important exam where you've studied your heart out, know everything there is to know, yet just before you enter the exam hall or turn the exam over, your mind goes blank?

Well, that's what happened to me.

And similarly, this can occur when the first half of a book has flown for me, then I reach the dreaded 'sagging middle' and...nada. My characters don't have a clue what happens next and neither do I.

It can happen if I've been so wrapped up in maintaining tension throughout a book, upping the stakes with each scene, that when I almost reach the end and the characters have the opportunity to resolve their differences, my mind has blanked.

There is so much that needs to be tied up all nice and tidily in one neat book that my brain refuses to co-operate.

So how to get around it?

Step 1: Write.

May sound simplistic but that's exactly what I have to do: write. Let the words flow. Do what I've done for the rest of the book. I can always go back and fix and layer later. Can't fix a blank page.

Step 2: Focus on obvious resolution.

Work on one problem at a time. Don't stress about tying up the rest of the loose ends. Leave this for the first revision pass, where you can jot down the threads that need tying as you re-read the book and follow up at the end.

Step 3: Think happy thoughts.

My characters have waited all book to get their Happily Ever After. Don't cheat them. Make this scene a cracker so you leave your readers craving more (and rushing out to the bookstore when your next release hits the shelves!)

Step 4: The fantasy of romance.

We all love sigh-worthy romantic endings but if you've had a strong conflict throughout the book, resolving differences isn't always easy. Therefore, concentrate on making this final scene real. If all can be solved with a simple conversation, then the odds are your conflict throughout the book hasn't been strong enough.

Step 5: Finish at all costs.

I like my books to flow in one, cohesive block. I don't jump around from scene to scene (though many writers do.) I write the first draft in one go then go back and layer. When I'm stuck, I want to go back and read what I've written before finishing the book. But I don't. Why?

I want the ending to be instinctive, like the rest of the book has been. I want it to flow on from the last scene, and not be contrived from something I've written earlier. I want it to be a natural resolution of everything that has happened before.

Plenty of time to tweak later.

That's what editing and revisions are for.

TYPING 'THE END'

Surely there is no greater feeling than typing those two little words when you finish slogging over your pride and joy?

'THE END'.

Finished. Done. Complete.

After all the hard work, all the inspiration, battling the sagging middle, nutting out the internal conflicts, getting your characters to resolve their differences and creating a happily-ever-after that is truly sigh-worthy, there is no greater feeling than typing those two tiny magical words.

For many of us, we can take our time doing all of the above. But what if you don't have that luxury? What if writing you're writing to meet a deadline?

Here are a few things that work for me:

CLOCK WATCHING

When I'm on deadline, fairly constant these days considering I write for 4 publishers, I'm a self-confessed clock-watcher. What this means for me is that I only have a small window of opportunity to write each day due to family commitments so I make the most of that time. If you have 2 hours a day, make the most of every minute. If you have 10 minutes a day, make the most of every second. Many writers swear by egg timers, where you set your allocated time limit for the day and write like mad, only stopping when the buzzer goes off. For me, it's enough to glance at the clock, know I only have 15 minutes left and off I go, trying to get to the end of the next scene before tomorrow.

GOAL SETTING

If you only have a limited time to write a book (e.g. a month) it is much easier to set achievable goals with the time you have. For example, if you can average 10 pages a day and write 5 days a week, you know that you'll get that book done in a month. Breaking down the monstrous task into bite-size chunks can take the pressure off (or at least give you a false sense of security!)

MAKE THE MOST OF EVERY SECOND

If you're anything like me, you don't often get a spare second to yourself. That's life. However, one thing I've learned to do when on deadline is making the most of any unexpected time. Keep a notebook handy while you're waiting to pick up the kids; outlining your next scene in dot points can save precious time later. Waiting at the checkout? Ditto. Dinner under control? An extra five minutes at the PC can make those words add up.

ME TIME

'What's that?' I hear many of you scream in outrage and I hear you. However, working to deadline is tough work and mentally draining so to keep yourself in top form during this stressful time you need time out.

You're a caffeine addict? Grab regular coffees *away* from the keyboard.

Like to devour books? Read a chapter to unwind, inspire, whatever, but read for enjoyment not research.

Without quality 'me time' you run the risk of burn-out and there's no way that book will get finished, deadline or not, if that happens, so look after yourself.

MOVE IT OR LOSE IT

I was a physiotherapist in a previous life and while I'm a lazy person at heart and not into exercise at all (don't tell all those poor patients I badgered to exercise!) I strongly urge you to move regularly while writing. Long, unbroken stints at the computer may result in chronic postural problems- and pain-so to effectively meet the demands of deadlines, take regular breaks away from the PC, even if it's to stretch a few times before planting your butt back in the chair.

MOTIVATION

For me, meeting deadlines is a cinch when I'm motivated. Considering I have a mortgage and bills to pay while also paying for my kids' education, I'm extremely motivated all the time.

Of course, it's nice to dream that one day I'll be writing my books while lying under a palm tree with a hot cabana boy to fan me, so that's pretty motivating too!

Writing to deadline is hard work, so whatever works for you, do it.

STAND OUT FROM THE CROWD

After hours of hard slog, blood, sweat and tears, you've finally typed 'The End' on your brilliant manuscript. Now, where to from here? Should you post it away to those editors eager to offer you a contract immediately? Should you give it to your mum/sister/best friend to read? Has it been critiqued/reviewed/edited to death?

If you've answered yes to all of the above, it's time to polish your masterpiece and make it **STAND OUT** from the crowd to grab that acquiring editor's attention.

Strength

Your characters have been whispering their story to you throughout the book and you think you've done a fine job getting their tale down. However, have your hero and heroine got a strong individual voice? Strong individual characteristics that make them different from your secondary characters? And most importantly, a strong emotional conflict to keep the readers turning the pages of your novel to the very end?

To gain perspective on your work and be able to objectively answer the questions above, set it aside for a few weeks before returning to edit. You'll be amazed at what you pick up after distancing yourself from the story.

Timing

We've all heard the saying "timing is everything." In the case of your story, it's crucial. Make sure the story's events are chronological and follow a natural time progression. There is nothing as distracting as back flipping the pages of a novel in confusion as a winter bride frolics in the autumn leaves with her new groom a chapter later.

Don't make an editor stop reading your manuscript for a second. You want that editor riveted to your every word, turning pages fast to reach the guaranteed happily ever after, and using her precious time to devour your story, the story she wants to buy.

Attitude

Sassy, bold, brazen. Whichever term you prefer, make sure your heroine has it in spades—and then some. Make your heroine likeable, identifiable and most of all, human. Give her endearing faults, funny traits, whatever it takes, just make sure she has loads of appeal that readers will love.

Nous

How many times have we slammed a book shut after the first few pages in frustration because the heroine is TSTL (too stupid to live)? Women today are strong-willed, street-smart individuals and if you're writing a contemporary romance, your heroine needs to have these characteristics. Give her enough nous to stand up to that hero and give as good as she gets. Your readers will love you for it.

Depth

Give your story depth. Don't pad it with pages of waffle such as unnecessary back-story, boring internal POV and mindless dialogue that doesn't further the action, all in the name of making a word count.

When in doubt, cut. If you're bored with a particular paragraph, guaranteed an editor will be too.

Depth of characters will accentuate the depth of the story. Give your characters layers, make them as human as possible and allow them to leap off the page screaming, "I'm here. And I'm lovable."

Organize

Your manuscript is near on perfect and you're itching to send it off. Whoa! Hold on a minute. Have you taken the time to check the agent/publisher's guidelines? Are the font, spacing and pagination what they're after? Editors receive thousands of unsolicited manuscripts a year and you want yours to stand out from the crowd, remember? Give yourself every advantage and make your story look as professional as possible.

Unique

Is there one thing that makes your story stand out from the crowd? Is it a new twist on an old theme? An unusual take on a tried and true plot? A killer heroine? Whatever it is, highlight it. Whether it be in the first paragraph of your query letter or synopsis, make sure that editor takes one look at your highly original concept and says 'more'!

Trends

You've written the dream book, the one that flies from

your fingertips onto the computer screen with little effort, your critique partner thinks it's perfect and you have a gut feeling that this is 'the one' that's going to launch you from writer to published author.

This book may be 'the one' but if the theme or premise of the book is out of date, an editor may have to pass in favor of another manuscript that highlights the trends of current bestsellers.

The easiest way to keep abreast of trends is to read. May sound obvious but when I first started writing and targeting Mills and Boon, I hadn't read one since I was a teenager. My first book had a theme involving speed dating, a modern topic at the time, and my editor told me when I got 'the call' that the unusual take on a modern theme drew her in from the start.

Another example is Bridget Jones's Diary. Helen Fielding tapped into the universal themes of modern women everywhere: being single, overweight, turning up to family functions partner-less...haven't many of us been there?

So, as much as you want your book to stand out from the crowd, following that crowd every now and then isn't such a bad idea.

MANUSCRIPT STEW

Take one first draft.
Well done.
Leave to stew for a week, minimum.
Then take one pair of fresh eyes, one pair of eager hands with itchy fingers to type and a fresh perspective.
Re-open first draft and start the editing process.

Sounds easy, right?

Wrong!

If you're like me, it's hard to walk away from a manuscript, especially one just finished. Though exhausted, your mind is still buzzing with ideas, you're still in the characters' heads, the setting is still vivid and you want to get this baby off to an editor/agent/submission pile ASAP.

Instead, let it stew.

The longer the better.

There's nothing like tackling a first draft with a

completely fresh outlook, and with the benefit of time away from the story.

It's too easy to get caught up in your plot or be too close to your characters and after a while you can't see the pitfalls, the holes and the glaring mistakes. This is why time away is essential, especially if you don't have a critique partner to pick up this stuff for you in later drafts.

Fresh eyes bring fresh perspective, an eagerness to layer, and the all-important clarity to make your story the best it can be.

So do what I do.

Immerse yourself in the rest of your life.

Keep busy.

Recover from those sleepless nights while immersed in your story.

Read.

Watch TV.

Have fun.

And then take those itching fingers back to the keyboard and start the writing process all over again.

LAYERING AND EDITING

It's done.

You've finished your manuscript and allowed it to stew.

Now it's time for the all important layering and editing phase.

I consider layering to be the cream, jam and icing you add to a basic sponge.

Layering adds richness, a depth to your first draft.

It allows you to develop a scene/character/setting, bringing it to life.

Think about your characters in a particular scene:

What do they hear?

Feel?

Taste?

Smell?

Are there noises around? Other people?

Use a bit of lovely description to bring the scene alive.

I'm not advocating adding a heap of adjectives but going through your manuscript with a keen eye for detail and bringing it to life.

Here's an example from BRASH.

Jess pushed through a phalanx of fuchsia feather fans and slipped into the main dressing room, only to be confronted by nudity.

"Jeez, put some clothes on," she said, unable to resist brushing against the vermillion velvet walls as she entered. The plushness of this room never failed to bring out her inner vixen.

"Don't like the view? You know where the door is." Zazz, Burlesque Bombshell's premier dancer, leaned closer to the gilt edged, beveled mirror and puckered up, before slicking vivid crimson across her lips.

"Not a problem. But then who'd plan your gargantuan wedding, huh?" Jess picked up an armful of feather boas and draped them over a mannequin before slouching on a plush peacock blue suede daybed. "Wedding of the century, babe. Your quote, not mine."

"Whatever." Zazz batted her eyelash extensions and pouted. "Table arrangements finalized?"

"Yep. Ruby linen tablecloths. Matching chairs tied with black bows. Elongated glass vases filled with ebony crystals and long feathers. Silverware. Black candles. And bling name holders—"

"Whoa. Detail overload." Zazz held up her hands. "As long as it matches the pics of that swank London Goth wedding you showed me in a bridal mag, I'm happy."

"Easy to please." Jess used her hand as a fake notebook and jotted with an imaginary pen. "Not."

Through a subtle layering of adjectives throughout this short snippet, richness is added that gives the reader a feel for the setting.

-fuchsia feather fans

-vermillion velvet walls
-gilt-edged beveled mirror
-plush peacock blue suede daybed

Here's another snippet from BRASH, layering in smell.

She stopped less than a foot away, invading his personal space, too damn close. He could smell a hint of her lilac shampoo overlaid with something stronger, something more potent.

Desire.

He was a dead man.

And another example from BRASH, where less is more.

Jack filled her senses. He tasted like bourbon. He smelt like heaven. He felt like sin.

You don't need to add a lot of words to layer richness or add impact. Less is more can be powerful.

With editing, it is more than doing a grammar and spell check.

Have you chosen the best word possible?

Have you used hooks at the end of your chapters?

Have you maintained POV and not jumped around within a scene?

Does the dialogue flow? Have you watched overuse of tags?

Have you checked for oft-repeated, overused words?

Have you read through your work more than once?

You'd be amazed how errors can slip by tired eyes. Trust

me, I know! Working at night, finishing edits at the end of a week, can make for very tired eyes...

This is by no means a definitive list of things to watch for, and there are loads of fantastic resources to help you with the editing process. So spend a bit of time searching the Internet or scouring your local bookshop, and put in the hard yards to discover the techniques that make your manuscript shine.

I know some authors print their completed manuscript out and go through it with a highlighter or red pen, marking all or some of the above.

I work from the computer screen direct; it works for me.

Do what works for you.

If you get to the layering/editing stage, you've done well.

You've finished your first draft. You now have something solid to work with, a story to fiddle and fine tune into a masterpiece.

THE WAITING GAME

The publishing industry revolves around waiting.

Waiting for an editor/agent to read our first partial.

Waiting for an editor/agent to read our first full.

Waiting for competition results.

Waiting for 'the call'.

Waiting for our first set of revisions.

Waiting to hold our first book in our hot little hands.

Waiting for it to hit the shelves.

Waiting for reviews.

Waiting for sales figures, royalties, approval on our next proposal...

I'll give it to you straight.

Even once you're published, you still have to wait.

And yes, it's perfectly normal to wait by the front door for the postman to bring you a lovely box of your next books, to frantically refresh your inbox while waiting to hear from your editor for news on your latest submission, to run for the phone when you're expecting a call about your next contract.

So what can you do to make the wait easier?

Start thinking about/plotting/outlining your next book. Nothing like the thrill of a new book to get you focused on something other than waiting.

Start writing your next book. This has the added bonus of having something else to show your editor when you get the call and she asks if you have anything else in the pipeline. Editors are looking to build your career as an author, not to buy a single book, so keep writing.

Get your creative juices flowing. Pick up a new magazine. Watch a new TV show. Go out and people watch. Let your ideas flow and don't forget to jot them down for future storylines.

Read. Indulge in your favorite author or better yet, pick up a new one. Reading is research and a great way to wait.

Research. Nothing better to get the hours flying by than delving into the wonderful world of research. Let the Internet or local library take you on a magical journey of facts.

Resources. Bought a stack of 'how to' books but never have the time to check them out? Now is that time. While waiting, hone your writing skills, making your next book even better.

Hope these tips help you pass the time wisely.

TEACHING AN OLD MANUSCRIPT NEW TRICKS

Do you have an old manuscript lying in a draw or on your PC somewhere?

Ever wondered what it would be like to dust it off, polish it and sell it? Or in today's ever evolving publishing industry, indie pub it?

Here are a few pointers to help you revamp an old manuscript:

REVAMP YOUR CHARACTERS

You don't need to change your characters' personalities as such but I do recommend a change of name. It's a small change that gives an old manuscript a new feel.

I also choose new pictures to represent my characters. A re-casting will ensure the characters get a new lease on life.

The story may essentially be the same but by freshening your characters in any way you can will give the story a much needed overhaul.

DO A FULL READ THROUGH

Before you start rewriting, I recommend doing a full

read through of the old manuscript. It gives you perspective of the overall story, where it might be falling down, if any motivations need to be changed and a general feel of where you want to go.

It's also an eye-opening experience to see how your writing has developed, strengthened and clarified, in some cases over years.

CLARIFY NEW MOTIVATIONS/CONFLICTS

Get these straight in your head, jot them down on paper, whatever, but be clear the direction you want this revamped edition to take. Otherwise, you could find yourself half way through the book and dithering between the old conflict and the new. Be clear from the start and you won't go wrong.

BE PREPARED TO SLASH

I love words. If you're a writer, you love words too. How they flow together, how they sound, the way they convey so much. However, if you're revamping, be prepared to get rid of words. Maybe lots of them.

I hate slashing. But it's amazing when you edit an old story how much you pick up that you can get rid of.

I recommend you keep slashed scenes in a 'deleted' folder. You never know when one book's trash can become another book's treasure.

OUT WITH THE OLD, IN WITH THE NEW

After you've slashed the extraneous bits you'll need to write the new scenes and this requires some serious layering.

You want the book to flow.

You want it to seem like you've written the whole thing

in one seamless stream even if most of it was written years earlier.

Careful layering will achieve this and that's why I recommend a thorough read-through at the start. You must be familiar with the plot, with the characters and their motivations to affectively layer in the new after the old has hit the deleted file.

POLISH

We all know that once you've finished writing a story you need to let it sit and ferment for a while before approaching it with fresh eyes to do the final polish/edit.

This final step is particularly important in revamping an old manuscript as it gives you added perspective to pick up any disjointed sections where your layering hasn't been spot on.

So let the manuscript rest. Give it some time. 5-7 days usually works for me, as I can't afford to give it longer because of other deadlines, but longer is better.

Good luck in teaching an old manuscript new tricks. Try it. You'll be surprised how much fun it can be and if it results in a sale, even better.

(FAKING IT is an example of one of my books that underwent a serious 'out with the old, in with the new' during revision stages. Many readers have commented it reads seamlessly, which means I've done my job right, considering I slashed some old scenes and layered many new ones through the manuscript six years after it was originally written.)

REVISIONS

What do revisions entail?

They can be quite detailed, from the editor picking up something specific and quoting from a page number to a broader 'the emotional tension needs to be ramped up between these two.'

They tend to focus around specific areas of the story: plot, character, emotional conflict.

They tighten the story in ways you can't imagine.

They pick up any contradictions in your characters' behavior throughout the story.

They focus on the good stuff in your story and show you ways to make it better.

When I first get revisions from an editor, I'm nervous.

They always look more daunting than they are. Often pages and pages of what needs to be fixed in the story!

Even after 80 books, seeing what needs to be cut/expanded/deepened makes me want to hide.

So what to do when revisions land?

Read them.

Print them out.

Let them sit a while, usually a day.

Take a deep breath and re-read.

Go over key points with a highlighter.

Make a list of things to watch for as you re-tackle the manuscript.

I tick off key points as I cover them during the revision process, just to make sure I've done everything.

Remember that revisions are one person's viewpoint (a very important person, mind you, if you want to sell the book!) and if you don't agree with something discuss it with your editor.

Flesh out the problem.

Throw a few ideas around.

Your manuscript will be better for it.

RESILIENCE

Publishing is a fluid industry.

Ever-changing, challenging, trends come and go.

As an author, how do you survive?

Resilience.

It's a quality schools strive to instil in kids.

About learning how to cope with hard knocks.

About moving on when things don't go your way.

About adapting.

About learning to forge ahead when things are against you.

Here's a publishing example:

When I first sold to Harlequin, I went on to publish 45 books in 16 years. Some assume that once you get a contract with Harlequin Mills and Boon that you can keep writing for them for infinity.

Hmmm...myth.

The reality for me? I had 8 editors and they were all brilliant but after I had my first child I wrote 2 books in 8 weeks.

Yes, you read that correctly.

Maybe it was being high on happy hormones?

Maybe the lack of sleep?

Maybe because I'd worked full time until then and suddenly had loads of time on my hands while baby slept?

Whatever the reason, I wrote those books and thought they were brilliant.

And they didn't sell.

I'd had a change of editor and those books didn't fly.

So what did I do?

Worked on a few proposals, found one she liked and wrote that book instead.

That book too was on the verge of rejection but I knew I could revise it so I did massive revisions and it sold.

After selling 5 books with barely a revision, those 2 rejections could've knocked me down. I could've stopped writing and bemoaned the fact I'd never sell another book.

Instead, I used the experience to spur me on.

I wanted to take my writing to the next level.

Another example is my women's fiction/rural romance novel LONG WAY HOME published with Harper Collins/Harlequin MIRA Australia. Initially, this book was rejected by the acquiring editor, who I'd met at a conference and connected with. But when my agent sent that rejection, I read through it and realized it sounded like a revision letter. So I asked if I could revise, taking the suggestions onboard, and resubmit. The result? The book sold for a decent advance on a 2 book contract. I could've given up after the initial rejection but I didn't. I knew my story had potential and I wanted to share it with readers so I put in the hard work to make that happen.

Resilience = how we cope when the going gets tough.

Once you're published, there is no magical fairy

godmother that waves a wand over all your manuscripts and makes them instantly publishable.

You still need to work at it.

You still need to produce your best work time and time again to secure more contracts.

You still need to keep striving.

I do.

Every single day when I sit down at my keyboard I want to prove to myself I can still do this, that I can go one better.

It's what drives me. What keeps me writing when the trends change and sales you expect don't materialize and the book of your heart isn't what's hot right now.

There are loads of resources to learn writing craft.

Only you can refine resilience.

(PS. Those 2 rejected manuscripts? Reworked and sold a few years later. One was DATE ME, a USA TODAY bestseller, a Romantic Times Magazine Top Pick and a RT Reviewers' Choice Award finalist.

Another of my mottos? Never say never!)

COPING WITH CHANGE

If there's one thing surer in the publishing game, you have to get used to change.

Absolutely love that title you've chosen? Odds are, it will get changed.

Love the hero who has inspired the book and sure you'll get a look-a-like for your cover? Uh-uh, will probably get changed.

Adore your editor and think she's the best thing since the last Susan Elizabeth Phillips novel? Editors have lives too and move on/get promoted/get wanderlust/get pregnant/etc.... change is inevitable.

So how do you deal with change?

Firstly, writing is a business. Treat it as such. In the business world, staff turnover is a given and we get used to fare-welling colleagues and bosses.

In the writing world, I think it's harder saying goodbye because our editor becomes our champion and we have a closer relationship than some of our colleagues.

Secondly, it's a small world. No matter how much you love your editor and want to fling yourself at her feet and beg her to stay, resist the urge, wish her well, act professional.

You never know when she'll become the CEO of the next publishing company you sell to and will remember your pathetic sniveling.

Thirdly, remain focused. Writing and reading is subjective so a book I love you may hate. This can apply to anyone, editors included, so it's natural to harbor a little anxiety that your new editor may not love your work as much as you do.

The key to dealing with this is staying focused, keep writing, keep producing the best books you can. Worrying about something you can't control is wasted energy and we'd rather be super productive, right?

Lastly, be flexible. The publishing industry ebbs and flows. Trends come and go, people come and go, authors come and go.

Publishers change, guidelines change, series change.

Writing is all about being able to adapt, to staying true to your voice even when faced with the inevitable change.

After all, our distinctive writing voice is the one thing we can't change.

And remember, if all else fails as a coping mechanism for change, there's always chocolate...

MOTIVATION

You've had the brilliant idea.

You're going to write a book.

The words fly from your fingers for the first chapter, the first three chapters, maybe the first six chapters.

Then what?

Life intrudes.

Your kids need more attention than usual, your extended family descends to stay for a while, your day job turns manic, you're exhausted and the last thing you feel like is sitting at the computer and writing.

This is where a little healthy motivation comes in handy.

So what motivates me?

DEADLINE

There's nothing like a looming date on a contract you've already signed to get those fingers flying. If you're unpublished, set your own personal deadline: before the end of the year, before Spring, whenever, and stick to it. Get a feeling for pressure, what it feels like to write under those conditions. You might surprise yourself with the result. And best of all, it is great practice for when you are published.

MONEY

Yes, I'm being honest and money has to factor into it. In our family, I have to work for us to be economically viable and that means I have to sit in front of the computer every day and some nights too, when I'd rather be curled up in bed catching up on some much needed sleep. Paying bills, mortgage, school fees, whatever, is a great motivator.

SEEING MY NAME ON A BOOK

Am I vain? Maybe. But I'd be lying if I didn't say that each and every time I see my name on a book I've written, I get a little shiver down my spine. It's the most amazing feeling in the world and I will never, ever tire of it. Some unpublished writers make up mock covers. Place them on a corkboard. Have them as a screensaver.

My advice is to visualize your first cover and strive for it. Do everything in your power to make it happen and that usually means writing, writing and more writing.

REWARDS.

Many authors buy themselves a special present with each book. I started doing that and it really was great but somehow it fell by the wayside when I got wrapped up in kids clothing, school fees, swimming lessons, etc....

As part of goal setting, rewards can play an important part of finishing a book. It can be something as simple as your favorite cake for reaching the half way mark or a pair of spectacular shoes for reaching the end but whatever it is, make sure it's enough to drag your butt to the keyboard when you don't feel like it.

APPEASING THE SENSES

While I adore music, I can't listen to it while writing. But I know many authors who have a special soundtrack for every book they write.

While I love my food, I can't eat while I'm writing. Yet other authors have chocolate on hand at all times.

Keeping your muse happy with food, music, aromatherapy oils, whatever. It can go a long way to ticking over that word count.

BUST THROUGH THE ROADBLOCK

Sometimes it's hard to stay motivated when you're stuck.

We all know the feeling well: the first chapters fly, maybe the whole first half of the book, then we get hit by the sagging middle.

How do you stay on top of it?

How do you get past the roadblock to creativity?

For me, I focus on that last word: ***creativity***.

I sit with a blank sheet of paper and pen, and let the ideas flow.

Where can my characters go from here?

What can up the stakes?

Why are they behaving this way?

What will propel them towards the happily-ever-after they deserve?

Who has the most to lose?

What events can conspire against them?

What events can bring them closer together and up the tension?

These are just a few ideas to get you thinking.

I always find pen and paper extremely useful for 'unblocking'.

When I use this method, I also tend to end up outlining the rest of the book, even if it's only a line or two for each chapter.

You'd be amazed how much easier it is to finish the book with something solid to refer to when your mind (or characters) start wandering again.

Hope this helps get you past those mini blocks.

BEING A HYBRID

In Australia, hybrids are becoming more popular.

Cars, that is.

But when I first heard the term applied to authors by Bob Mayer at the RWAustralia conference in Melbourne 2011, have to admit I was fascinated.

By definition, hybrid means heterogeneous: 'diverse', 'composed of different elements'.

And that's what I wanted for my publishing career.

I love writing romance, women's fiction, domestic suspense and young adult novels. I'm a passionate reader of all and have a ball creating stories for adults and teens.

So how did I morph from writing category romances for Harlequin to adding other publishers to my writing portfolio and indie books?

By researching. A lot.

With the booming e-book market and a range of new publishers, I spent countless hours scouring online: Publishers Marketplace, Predators and Editors, Absolute Write forums, respected blogs, trusty google, following through on every link.

Yeah, it was a massive time suck but I considered it investing in my new hybrid future.

Through Publishers Marketplace, I discovered well-known, well-respected agents selling to new publishers I hadn't heard of. I investigated them and liked what I saw. I sold books to some. I took a chance. Because they're indicative of the exciting choices authors have, an array of opportunities that continue to expand with publishers launching digital series.

It's heady stuff for a hybrid!

So after traditionally publishing 35 books, why did I go indie?

Because a hybrid author enjoys the challenge of diversifying.

I've watched the evolution of indie-publishing with great interest. Bookmarked blogs by authors in the know, joined indie loops, filed away snippets, continued to build a social network. Scoured Amazon top 100 lists checking out covers, learned the intricacies of Kindle Unlimited versus Smashwords, asked questions. Found a fantastic formatter and a brilliant cover artist and editors with great insight. Then more recently, discovered the joys of doing it myself with Vellum.

Once again, this takes time but it's an investment in my hybrid future, because however my books are released, whether in print or ebook, with a traditional publisher or indie, my name is on that cover and I want my brand to be universal.

I want readers to know when they pick up a Nicola Marsh contemporary romance they're getting fun and flirty. Consistency is key and brand is important regardless of format or publisher.

So while I continue to juggle my contracts with traditional publishers, I still keep an eye on my indie books with the aim to expand my booklist.

After all, there's nothing a hybrid author enjoys more than juggling constant deadlines, family, kids and life, all on minimal sleep!

(Best tip for hybrid authors: dust bunnies will breed regardless of cleaning so ignore.)

WRITING RESOURCES

I wish you happy writing, copious words, speedy publication and mega sales.

Here is an abbreviated list of some excellent resources:

FLIP DICTIONARY by Barbara Ann Kipfer

BUILDING BELIEVABLE CHARACTERS by Marc McCutcheon

THE WRITER'S GUIDE TO CHARACTER TRAITS by Linda N. Edelstein

SELF-EDITING FOR FICTION WRITERS by Renni Browne and Dave King

CREATING UNFORGETTABLE CHARACTERS by Linda Seger

WRITING THE BREAKOUT NOVEL by Donald Maass

THE SYNONYM FINDER by J.I. Rodale

THE PLOT THICKENS by Noah Lukeman

45 MASTER CHARACTERS by Victoria Lynn Schmidt

STORY ENGINEERING by Larry Brooks

THE EMOTIONAL WOUND THESAURUS by Angela Ackerman and Becca Puglist

(Now in an online version: ONE STOP FOR WRITERS)

BREAK INTO FICTION by Mary Buckham and Dianna Love

SAVE THE CAT by Blake Snyder

FREE BOOK AND MORE

SIGN UP TO NICOLA'S NEWSLETTER for a free book!

Read Nicola's newest feel-good romance **DID NOT FINISH**

The **CREATIVE IN LOVE** series

THE GRUMPY GUY

THE SHY GUY

THE GOOD GUY

The **BASHFUL BRIDES** series

NOT THE MARRYING KIND

NOT THE ROMANTIC KIND

NOT THE DARING KIND

The **WORLD APART** series

WALKING THE LINE (FREE!)

CROSSING THE LINE

TOWING THE LINE

BLURRING THE LINE

WORLD APART BOXED SET

The **HOT ISLAND NIGHTS** duo

WICKED NIGHTS

WANTON NIGHTS

Try the **BOMBSHELLS** series

BEFORE (FREE!)

BRASH

BLUSH

BOLD

BAD

BOMBSHELLS BOXED SET

The **BOLLYWOOD BILLIONAIRES** series

FAKING IT

MAKING IT

The **LOOKING FOR LOVE** series

LUCKY LOVE

CRAZY LOVE

SAPPHIRES ARE A GUY'S BEST FRIEND

THE SECOND CHANCE GUY

Check out Nicola's website for a full list of her books.

And read her other romances as NIKKI NORTH.

'MILLIONAIRE IN THE CITY' series.

LUCKY

COCKY

CRAZY

FANCY

FLIRTY

FOLLY

MADLY

ESCAPE WITH ME series.

DATE ME

LOVE ME

DARE ME

TRUST ME

FORGIVE ME

LAW BREAKER series

THE DEAL MAKER

THE CONTRACT BREAKER

ABOUT THE AUTHOR

USA TODAY bestselling and multi-award winning author Nicola Marsh writes page-turning fiction to keep you up all night.

She's published 80 books and sold 8 million copies worldwide.
She currently writes contemporary romance and domestic suspense.

She's a Waldenbooks, Bookscan, Amazon, iBooks and Barnes & Noble bestseller, a RBY (Romantic Book of the Year) and National Readers' Choice Award winner, and a multi-finalist for many awards.

A physiotherapist for thirteen years, she now adores writing full time, raising her two dashing young heroes, sharing fine food with family and friends, and her favorite, curling up with a good book!

EXAMPLES

Examples used in this book were taken from several of
Nicola's releases:
BRASH
CRAZY LOVE
NOT THE MARRYING KIND
FAKING IT

You can read the first chapters of each book here to get an
idea of how she incorporates some of her tips into her
contemporary romance work.

BRASH
CHAPTER ONE

Burlesque Bombshell Basics
Sexy on the inside translates to sexy on the outside.

Jess Harper was the first to admit, sex made her uncomfortable.

Not the act itself, despite the lackluster efforts by her

ex, but the paraphernalia that surrounded her every time she stepped into Burlesque Bombshell, her cousin's Vegas dance venue.

The nipple tassels and diamante thongs and shiny poles made her feel inadequate. Like all that overt sexiness screamed she was a failure in the boudoir. She wasn't. It was the dorks she allowed in there that needed lessons: Getting It On 101.

She pushed through a phalanx of fuchsia feather fans and slipped into the main dressing room, only to be confronted by nudity.

"Jeez, put some clothes on," she said, unable to resist brushing against the vermillion velvet walls as she entered. The plushness of this room never failed to bring out her inner vixen.

"Don't like the view? You know where the door is." Zazz, Burlesque Bombshell's premier dancer, leaned closer to the gilt edged, beveled mirror and puckered up, before slicking vivid crimson across her lips.

"Not a problem. But then who'd plan your gargantuan wedding, huh?" Jess picked up an armful of feather boas and draped them over a mannequin before slouching on a plush peacock blue suede daybed. "Wedding of the century, babe. Your quote, not mine."

"Whatever." Zazz batted her eyelash extensions and pouted. "Table arrangements finalized?"

"Yep. Ruby linen tablecloths. Matching chairs tied with black bows. Elongated glass vases filled with ebony crystals and long feathers. Silverware. Black candles. And bling name holders—"

"Whoa. Detail overload." Zazz held up her hands. "As long as it matches the pics of that swank London Goth wedding you showed me in a bridal mag, I'm happy."

"Easy to please." Jess used her hand as a fake notebook and jotted with an imaginary pen. "Not."

"You're snooty because I haven't told you the venue yet." Zazz sniggered. "Trust me, you're going to love it."

Jess didn't have to love it. In fact, she couldn't give a flying fig if the venue had rope swings hanging from the roof and chains from the chandeliers. The faster she was done doing this favor for her mom, who'd coerced her into planning this wedding from her sickbed, the faster she could figure out what she'd do with the rest of her life.

One thing Jess knew for sure; it wouldn't be helping Pam, her flamboyant mom, plan any more crazy weddings.

"And wait 'til you hear about the food." Zazz shrugged into an emerald satin kimono embroidered with topaz crystals. "Michelin starred. Exotic. To die for."

"Good. Faster I know about the cake, faster I can get onto the cake table decorations."

Zazz cinched the sash at her waist, accentuating her knockout hourglass figure. "The chef should be here shortly so you can sit down together and go over boring deets like which canapés go with which wines."

"Goody." Jess clapped her hands in fake excitement. Last thing she felt like doing today was collaborating with some temperamental, egotistical chef. Visiting her mom first thing had been bad enough. "Getting back to the venue. You know I can't finalize everything 'til I see the room, get a feel for the layout—"

"Relax. We're flying you and the chef out to the island end of the week."

"Island?" Jess's jaded soul couldn't help but perk up at the idea of a free trip to some exotic island. "Where?"

"Prince Island."

"Never heard of it." Not that Jess cared. Any place with island in the title? She was there with flip-flops on.

Zazz smirked. "That's because my darling fiancé owns the island. Six star resort and private villas. Totally exclusive. Invitation only."

Jess clutched her heart in mock shock. "Serious?"

Zazz laughed. "Yeah, who would've thought Dorian would be a romantic?"

Nothing the doting groom did would surprise Jess. Dorian Gibbs owned most of Nevada and ruled Vegas but held his coveted bachelorhood as the biggest prize. Until he'd attended a Bombshell soiree, taken one glimpse at Zazz and fallen head over heels.

Jess didn't believe in clichés but there was something undeniably electric when Dorian and Zazz were in the same room. Pity the odd lightning bolt or two couldn't strike her. She could do with a good jumpstart. Her love life was on par with her career—down the toilet.

"Dorian would gift you the world on a silver platter if he could."

"I'm worth it." Zazz wriggled her fingers into a white satin glove and rolled it up to her elbow, smoothing it before repeating the elegant action on the other arm. "You are too, hun, and you'd know it if you'd ever let me fix you up with one of his friends."

"I prefer my guy to be in the same decade."

"Bitch." Zazz laughed. "Trust me, there's something to be said for an older man." She shimmied her hips, complete with a few crude pelvic thrusts. "They have the moves and know how to use them."

Jess winced. "If that's an indication of Dorian's moves, you can keep them."

"And relish them twice a day." Zazz propped on the end

of her dresser and folded her arms. "Seriously, when's the last time you had a date?"

Jess opened her mouth to respond and Zazz rushed on, "One that didn't involve battery operated apparatus."

"I get out."

Zazz harrumphed. "Taking your mom to rehab doesn't count."

"She needs my help."

"She's had a stroke and is taking full advantage of the fact to have you at her beck and call." Zazz shook her head. "Don't get me wrong, I appreciate you stepping in to take over as my wedding planner. But Pam's milking this for all she's worth."

Didn't Jess know it. Sure, she felt sorry for her vibrant mom suffering a stroke that rendered her left side immobilized. And she didn't begrudge helping her. What she couldn't stand was the constant interference in her life when she'd escaped Pam's smothering years earlier.

They may live in Craye Canyon, an hour out of Vegas, but that's where the similarities between her life and her mom's ended.

Pam went through boyfriends like coffee filters. She pranced around town in mini skirts and tube tops, had her hair blow-waved daily and cleaned out the town's cosmetic supply on a regular basis. She planned weddings with panache and style, at odds with her loud, brash self.

Little wonder Jess had chosen an occupation far removed from her mom's flamboyance. Town librarian was staid, unassuming and quiet. It suited Jess just fine. Until she'd heard rumors the local council considered Craye Canyon Library a dead loss and would downsize soon, so she saved them the trouble and quit, leaving her jobless and directionless.

In a way, planning Zazz's wedding had given her breathing space to decide where she went from here. One thing Jess knew, she was tired of her boring life. Sick to death of it. Zazz was right. She needed to shake things up a little.

"You need an island fling." Zazz snapped her fingers, her grin positively evil. "Hot stud. Sun, surf, sex."

Sounded pretty damn perfect. "And here I was, thinking you were flying me to some island to plan your wedding."

Zazz waved away her concern. "It'll happen, I have full confidence in you."

"The wedding or the sex?"

"Both." Zazz's eyes narrowed as she smirked. "How do you like your eggs in the morning?"

"Huh?"

"The chef?" Zazz fanned her face. "Unbe-freaking-lievable. Sex on legs."

"Yeah, right." Jess rolled her eyes. "Those black and white checkered pants do it for me every time."

Zazz laughed. "Trust me, once you get a look at this guy, those ugly pants won't be staying on for long."

"Chefs aren't my type."

The moment the lie tumbled from Jess's lips, memories long suppressed flashed before her eyes.

An outback holiday in Australia. A cattle station cook. A kiss that defied belief. And a refusal that burned, real bad.

Jack McVeigh graced TV screens the world over these days, a constant reminder of what she'd once wanted and couldn't have. With that bad boy stubble, murky green eyes and lazy smile, no great surprise he'd won the hearts of viewers glued to his gourmet cooking show with the same ease he'd won hers.

Pity the celebrity chef preferred to break hearts along with eggs.

"Trust me, babe. If this chef can't get into your panties, no one will."

Unease rippled down Jess's spine like a premonition. "Who's this mystery guy?"

Zazz glanced at her watch. "You'll see for yourself in five minutes. I asked him to meet us here."

Jess ignored the persistent tingle that maybe, just maybe, Zazz's chef could be Jack.

Impossible, considering Jack was based in Sydney and had enough gigs to keep him busy into the next century. Yeah, she Googled him, so what?

Besides, Zazz had said the chef catering the wedding was an old friend of Dorian's so the guy had to be the same vintage.

She didn't know what bothered her more: the sliver of disappointment she wouldn't see Jack face to face after a decade or the inhuman leap of her libido at the thought of a little one-on-one island time with the sexy chef.

"I need to check my final show times with Chantal." Zazz slipped her dainty feet into a pair of marabou feather mules and tightened the sash on her robe. "I'll be back in time for our meeting."

"What's his name—" Jess called out to Zazz's retreating back, wishing she had half the hip wiggle the sassy dancer had.

When Jess walked, men didn't stumble or gawk. She didn't warrant second glances or come-ons. She achieved exactly what she wanted to—anonymity and serenity, two qualities far removed from her boisterous, cringe-worthy mom.

With a sigh, she stood and wandered around the room,

her fingertips stroking the satins and silks, savoring the lush fabrics she could never wear in a million years.

Her fingers snagged on a set of gold spangled pasties complete with sparkly-fringed tassels and she picked them up, held them over her nipples, and grimaced.

So not her.

"Hey Jess."

Shock ripped through the carefully constructed poise Jess had honed to a fine art over the years as her hands fell to her sides.

She'd envisaged her first meeting with Jack over the years. Kinda inevitable, with her brother Reid being his best mate.

In her scenarios, their first meeting after a decade didn't involve nipple pasties. Or a smoother-than-whisky voice that made her palms sweat, her skin prickle and her inner bombshell want to strip on the spot.

"Hey you."

Not quite the scintillating opening gambit she'd imagined. Then again, having this big, bronze Aussie cross the room to stand less than a foot away had thrown her brain into chaos and her body into meltdown.

"Nice tassels."

His fingertip toyed with the nipple tassels hanging limply in her hand and she stiffened.

In the past, she would've responded with a blush. But after what he'd done to her? The way he'd humiliated her? Not a chance in hell she'd give him the satisfaction of seeing her cave again.

She held them over her breasts, vindicated when those impossibly green eyes widened, the pupils constricting. "Care to see them on?"

He took a step back. "Don't play with fire."

She took a step forward. "Maybe I'm in the mood to get hot?"

He swore. "You and me? Not going to happen."

"So you've said before," she drawled, giving the tassels a twirl for good measure, reveling in his discomfort as he tore his gaze away from her breasts. "But a decade is a long time."

"Not frigging long enough," he muttered, casting a desperate glance at the door.

So she ramped up the tension.

"These?" She waved the tassels in his face, deliberately taunting. "Tip of the iceberg in my new wardrobe. You should see me in the purple suspenders and sheer, crotchless—"

"Enough." A low, warning growl she had no intention of obeying. "Is this the way you treated your fiancé? Not surprised he bolted."

Just like that, her bravado faded, replaced by the dogged insecurity that tainted her botched relationship with Max, and fury at Jack for judging her.

"Fuck you." She eyeballed him, willing away the incriminating tears stinging her eyes.

That's when she saw the glimmer of victory in his eyes and knew he'd deliberately insulted her to push her away, like he had ten years earlier.

He turned and headed for the door, but not before she heard his murmured, "Babe, you have no idea how much I wish for that."

CRAZY LOVE
CHAPTER ONE

Cupid's Dating Tips for the Enlightened Male

Acknowledge you don't look like George Clooney (and get over it.)

"I'm in love."

Sierra Kent ignored her loquacious BFF Belle and focused on her PC, her French manicured nails flying over the keyboard as she entered Love Byte's latest batch of dating applicants. "Sure you are, hon. It's where we live and it's—"

"What makes the world go round. Yeah, yeah, heard it all before."

Belle Adamson, her best friend since grade school, wandered behind the desk to peer over her shoulder. "Save the BS for your clients because I'm not buying it. Besides, I only said that to get your attention."

Sierra paused, surprised by Belle's bitter tone.

"What's up?"

Belle ignored the question, her green eyes widening as she stared at the computer screen.

"Who's *that*?"

"The agency's latest applicant." Sierra glanced at the photo she'd downloaded and wolf-whistled. "Pretty damn hot, huh?"

Belle fanned her face. "Any chance of matching me with him?"

"What happened to being in love?"

"I meant our town, obviously." Belle grinned, her gaze riveted to the screen. "Now start matchmaking."

Sierra laughed and erased the image of applicant 8049 with a tap on the delete key. "This is a dating agency, not a matchmaking service."

Belle arched a perfectly shaped eyebrow. "The difference is?"

"Fill out the forms like everyone else, let me input your info into trusty Cupid and his megabytes will statistically find you a suitable date." She snapped her fingers. "And hand over the hundred dollar fee like everyone else."

"What do I get for the matchmaking service?"

"A bottle of tequila, a push-up bra and free entry into Venus for a night?"

Belle screwed up her nose and perched on the edge of the desk. "I'm sick of the cowboys and out-of-towners in that joint. Besides," she patted the sides of her DD breasts and smirked like a woman well aware of her assets, "I get by on what the good Lord gave me. Though the tequila sounds like a plan."

"Mexican? My place at seven?"

"We talking food or a tall, dark, handsome stranger from south of the border?"

"That applicant was blond. Nice to know you're not fussy."

Belle slid off the desk, tugged her pastel pink beautician's uniform over her lush curves and picked up her handbag.

"With my luck lately I'd settle for a Martian."

"I hear it's not the size of the antenna that's important, it's the way the Martian wiggles it."

Belle performed an imaginary drum roll complete with cymbal crash. "An oldie but a goodie. Later, babe."

As Belle strolled out of the office working her hips, Sierra wondered why her gorgeous friend hadn't found love yet. Curvy, stacked blondes were always the rage yet Belle hadn't been serious about a guy since...ever.

Sierra put it down to the intimidation factor. Guys took one look at Belle's hot bod and movie star blonde bombshell attitude and bolted for the nearest cold shower and porno flick, not necessarily in that order.

And despite her interest in Love Byte, Belle had never let Sierra input her data into the computer. "*I'm not a desperado. Yet.*" Was her usual spiel but now she'd turned thirty, who knew?

Besides, it was difficult coping with single-dom when surrounded by Love. Ask the town's twelve thousand inhabitants who happily touted the emotion to anyone willing to listen.

And people did. Crowds flocked to the only place in the good ol' US of A that promised the often unattainable for those lucky enough to visit.

Personally, Sierra preferred LA for its hip vibe. Instead, she was stuck an hour south of the City of Angels, surrounded by kitschy reminders of an emotion she touted for a living but didn't believe in.

Dolores Kent did, which is why Sierra had been here since the age of ten, when her dad ran off and her mom settled in the hope of finding the fabled love the town promised. It never eventuated and Dolores now resided in Nepal trying to find nirvana on a higher plain.

Despite Sierra's initial loathing, the place had grown on her. Thanks to a stint on Letterman a few years back Love had blossomed with lonely hearts flocking in droves, eager to test the theory the town lived up to its name.

With Sierra's input, it did. She loved computers and loved people, and her passion for matchmaking had created Love Byte, one of California's largest Internet dating sites.

People thought it romantic to be matched in Love. She found it corny yet lucrative and she'd proudly watched her business grow from working out of her back room with a single computer and a few local applicants to an office, a plethora of virtual assistants and enough work to keep her in the designer gear she coveted.

It hadn't hurt when Hollywood's resident bad-boy Porter Davey, researching a part in his latest blockbuster romantic comedy about dating in the twenty-first century, had stumbled across her website. He'd plugged his name in as a joke, filled out an application and been totally blown away when matched with Jaime Sutton, the darling of the Australian tennis world.

Jaime, whose coach was a born and bred Lovernian, had entered her data into Love Byte's computer as part of a promotion to coincide with her first sponsorship deal with a Silicon Valley mega corporation, and Sierra hadn't removed it.

Neither Porter nor Jaime had minded her gaff and when the two met at her office where she'd called an emergency meeting to apologize for the mistake, they'd taken one look at each other and fallen head over heels.

She'd milked every drop of PR from the Davey-Sutton match and as a result had enough business to last into the next decade.

Sipping at her cappuccino, Sierra opened her sixtieth email for the afternoon, her attention momentarily snagged by yet another gorgeous guy with come-get-me eyes and a dimpled smile. Her job was tough but somebody had to do it and she tilted her head to one side, wondering if the picture had been Photo-shopped.

As she leaned forward for a closer look, the outer bell rang and she winced as the first few bars of "Can't Help Falling in Love with You" pealed out. The tacky factor always made her cringe but the customers loved it. And what the paying patrons loved she provided. She'd wasted enough years rebelling against the town and all it stood for before finally realizing if you can't beat 'em join 'em.

"I'll be with you in a sec," she called out, hitting 'save' before leaving her PC, having learned diligence the hard way via a computer crash in the early days that left her manic for a week.

Though it hadn't been all bad. The computer geek from LA had turned out to be anything but and they'd created a few wham-bam crashes of the horizontal kind while he'd been in town. Something she didn't usually do but hey, she'd always been a sucker for a kindred spirit and Mr. Motherboard had been a loner, one with nice pecs and dimples to boot. They'd flirted, they'd danced, they'd fooled around a bit.

The memory brought a smile to her face, which widened further as she caught a glimpse of her visitor.

Pity Belle hadn't stuck around because the guy inspecting the photos of married couples on her wall was the clichéd tall, dark and handsome in a big way.

"Can I help you?"

He turned, his piercing gaze making her skin prickle like she'd consumed an ocean's worth of shrimp, guaranteed to bring her out in hives.

His eyes were dark as coal, Superman eyes, able to penetrate concrete and women's outer layers of clothing with a single stare.

"I hope so. Nobody else in this town seems to know the meaning of the word."

Uh-oh. Not easy to place, these ones. They got a ten in the looks and body department but most women wanted a pleasant conversationalist too, not a grizzly with a temperament to match.

"I'm looking for the matchmaking woman. Is she

around?"

O-kay. Make that grizzly with a sore tooth.

Mustering her best placating smile, she held out her hand. "I'm Sierra Kent, owner of Love Byte."

He ignored her outstretched hand, his gaze flicking from head to foot as if assessing her credentials. "Figures."

Her hand dropped and she amended her summation to grizzly with a sore tooth and a bad case of PMS. Surely her *credentials* weren't that bad?

Only one way to handle an old grizzly: bait him further. Besides, she was all out of honey.

"You aren't here to fill out an application?"

The frown tattooed between his brows deepened. "I'm not here for a job, if that's what you mean."

Maybe old grizzly was plain dumb as well?

"This is a dating agency, Mr.? That's right, I didn't quite catch your name. Must've missed it along with the introductory hand shake."

His lips twitched with amusement. Nah...that would mean the guy actually had a sense of humor and from his dour expression, she doubted it.

"Marc Fairley."

Fairley? Surely he couldn't be related to the sweet lady her Uncle Hank was courting?

"I hear you've brainwashed my mother into believing the bull you spout here."

Great. Not only was Mr. High and Mighty related, he was Olivia Fairley's son?

Interfering relatives she could do without, especially ones that threatened her uncle's happiness. Hank was the one guy who had never let her down and if she could repay him in any way she'd do it.

He'd asked her to help organize the wedding, the first

time he'd ever asked her for anything and she would do everything in her power to make it happen.

As for grizzly, he'd have to get used to the fact his mother and Hank were tying the knot and butt out.

She gritted her teeth and forced a polite smile. "Mr. Fairley, I—"

"Call me Marc."

She hated interruptions, adding rude and condescending to his growing list of faults, and continued as if he hadn't spoken.

"I'm not sure what you've heard but I run a respectable business here. Your mother approached me in search of companionship and I've provided that for her."

"Save the spiel. I'm not one of your gullible singles."

"Your wife must be so proud," she muttered, resisting the urge to pick up the nearest object, which happened to be one of the elephants she collected, and fling it at him Frisbee-style. Nothing like a good tusk in the eye to prove a point.

He stiffened and thrust his hands into his pockets. "I'm not married. Not that it's any of your business."

"That's where you're wrong."

She sauntered to the front desk, throwing in an extra hip wiggle for the fun of it, picked up a folder and held it out to him.

"Making people happy is my business and if my services lead people to marriage? Bonus."

He didn't take the folder so the placed it in front of him and tapped it. "I can see where your problem lies. You're single and not enjoying it so check out my brochures, fill out the forms, and I can rectify that little problem for you in a second."

She snapped her fingers, struggling to keep a straight

face as his lips compressed, his dark gaze hard and uncompromising. She hadn't had this much fun in ages and baiting Marc Fairley could easily become a new pastime.

"Promise not to think you're *gullible*."

His face reddened, his neck muscles tensed and his eyes narrowed to angry slits. However, just when their discussion promised to get interesting, he surprised her.

"Fine. I'll look over your information and get back to you."

He grabbed the folder and stalked out the door, leaving her slightly disappointed. She'd expected more of a fight but grizzly had sheathed his claws and retreated.

Men like him, stimulating, challenging, with enough arrogance to keep her interested, didn't drop by every day and she'd hoped to get a few more barbs in before he left.

Shaking her head, she headed back to her desk and a pile of applications waiting for Cupid's expertise.

If a grumble-bum like Marc Fairley had sparked her interest she needed some serious downtime, preferably with a guy that wouldn't look down his snooty nose at her business or bite her head off every time she opened her mouth.

Or better yet, she could immerse herself in work, her usual panacea for all ills, including the lonely bug that crawled under her skin on the odd occasion.

She rummaged in her top drawer for a pen and came across an old Post-it note where Belle had scribbled "GOLF" and stuck it to the bottom of the drawer. Her friend's motto of "Guaranteed Orgasmic Laid-back Fun" hadn't steered Belle wrong so why couldn't she do the same?

Work was Sierra's usual excuse but if she were completely honest she didn't go for *laid-back fun*, Belle's euphemism for one night stands. Too brief, too impersonal, but isn't that what she wanted? Anything more was too complicated and if there was one thing she wasn't good at, it was complication. Her childhood years had been testament to that.

Besides, falling for a guy was *not* on her agenda, especially not now when her business was starting to take off. She had an enterprise to build and a seven-figure goal for her nest egg. No use relying on some guy to come along and provide her with security, a sure fire way to end up broke and alone when he ran out.

She'd watched her mom struggle financially and emotionally and it wasn't for her. She'd make her own way in this world and if a worthy guy came along to tempt her into thinking happily-ever-after, she'd consider it—before bolting in the opposite direction.

She could peddle love, she could live in a town where it slapped her in the face every day, she just couldn't go there herself. And when a first-class jerk like Marc Fairley walked into her office and she started thinking *laid-back fun*, she knew it was time for a major distraction, something to fill her time other than work.

Her fingers toyed with the Post-It. Maybe she should change her philosophy and give Belle's GOLF motto a try? Being in control and man-free had kept her sane, kept her grounded and warded off any potential threat to her ordered life for the last few years but was she satisfied?

She had great friends, a comfortable house, a successful business and Ripley, her beloved mutt—part Dane, part wolfhound.

A girl didn't need anything or anyone else, though the occasional date, drink, meal and GOLF might go a long way to staving off the loneliness that threatened occasionally. A girl couldn't live in Love and on fresh air alone.

Only problem was, she'd auditioned most of the half-decent guys in town for a GOLF game and had stopped well short of a hole-in-one every time. Apart from some heavy fooling around with Mr. Motherboard and a date with Belle's cousin Myron from Miami when he'd been in town an eon ago, she hadn't done much to hone her GOLF game in the last two years.

Pathetic, for a twenty-first century girl who collected more than elephants. Her stash of condoms had started out a joke but like anything else she did in life she liked to do it well. Despite her infrequent use of the product, she hoarded rubbers like some people saved stamps.

Belle had started the trend when a client had asked for a condom, and though Love Byte provided an all-inclusive dating service to its customers, Sierra had been unprepared for that request. Keen to remedy the situation, Belle had ordered an assortment of rubbers for the most discerning of daters and a new hobby had been born.

Belle was her major supplier, picking up the latest in condom couture whenever she hit the road on a buying trip for her salon. Sierra's current rubber raincoat stash? 367. Elephants? 105. No prizes for guessing where her priorities lay.

Now, the harder she tried to concentrate on work, the more her gaze flitted to that bright yellow Post-it and its message. And despite her best intentions to ignore it, she kept associating GOLF and Marc Fairley together in her head.

Stupid, stupid, stupid. She banged her head against her desk repeatedly, the position he found her in when he barged back into her office like a man possessed.

"You asked my mother about her *sexual preferences*?" Marc thrust the forms in her face and she shooed them away like a worrisome mosquito. "What sort of a sicko are you?"

She pushed against the floor with the tips of her pumps and swiveled back from the desk, hands behind her head as she leaned back.

"Nice to see you again, too."

"God-dammit. All I wanted was a little background info from you and I get this?"

He flung the papers on her desk and sank into the chair opposite, shaking his head from side to side. "You're a bigger pain in the ass than I anticipated."

So City Boy thought he could get the lowdown on his mom's relationship from her? Fat chance.

She blew him a kiss and batted her eyelashes. "Flattery will get you everywhere."

There it was again, the slight upturning at the corners of his mouth when she thought he'd give her a double-shot of that grizzly temper.

"If you extend those muscles around your mouth a fraction more you might actually crack it for a smile some day soon."

She flashed a dazzling smile as a demo.

"Are you this smart-mouthed with everyone who comes in here or is it just me?"

"It's you."

She wiggled her fingers in a cheeky wave, enjoying herself more by the minute, while he rubbed his temples as if staving off a blinder of a headache.

"What a frigging mess."

Bummer, just when she was getting warmed up to hurl some real insults his way, he had to tug on her heartstrings with his rendition of a man with the weight of the world on his oh-so-broad shoulders.

"Want to tell me about it?"

He fixed her with that Superman glare again, his hair doing the weird, spiky, just-out-of-bed thing guys' hair did, the thing she loved, especially if she got to run her hands through it and smooth down the spikes herself as they got back into bed.

Yikes. There she went again, associating grizzly with sex. Maybe she should give serious consideration to a round of GOLF sooner rather than later before she did something out of character, like making him her personal caddie and hope for a stroke under par.

"Long story. I'd rather not get into it."

He glanced at his Rolex and rubbed the spot between his eyes, the same one she would've been aiming for earlier if she'd gone through with her elephant throwing, where a tiny, perpetual frown resided. "Besides, I'm starving and I can't think on an empty stomach."

Oh no. No, no, *no*. She wasn't going to take up the challenge and invite him to have dinner with her. She already had plans with Belle. Mexican. Margaritas Tequila shots. *Sans* grumpy hot guy.

"Have some dinner then."

He stopped rubbing his forehead. "Is that an invitation?"

She should've feigned selective deafness. She should've said no. She should've ordered his uptight ass out of her office. Her lips formed a refusal.

"Whatever."

Great. She'd should've'd all over herself.

"I wouldn't want to put you out."

"You already did the minute you walked in here and started shooting off at the mouth but hey, never let it be said a Lovernian can't show an intruder some hospitality."

He smiled for the first time and the affect was breath-taking. It transformed his face, alleviating the hard planes, smoothing the frown and adding a depth she hadn't imagined. To make matters worse, he had a sexy crease in his right cheek and damn, she had a thing for dimples.

"Lovernian? You made that up, right?"

She looked away, unable to string coherent words together while he smiled like that.

"I wouldn't say that too loud around here. The local Lovernians are a species unto themselves and they devour stuck-up types like you for breakfast."

"You think I'm stuck-up?"

"I think you're a lot of things but let's not get into that now. I better save some abuse for dinner."

"Speaking of which, where do people eat in this hokey place?"

Don't invite him back to your place...don't invite him back to your place...

Thankfully, this time, her mind and mouth worked in sync.

"Chips'n'dips at Venus, the local bar, or home cooked stuff at the Love Shack. Take your pick."

His smile broadened to a grin and she sucked in a breath, blown away and trying not to show it. "Any other places around here named after dated songs? Guess I should gel my hair and squeeze into an old pair of acid-washed denim."

Great, now he was pulling out the big guns. Apart from dimples, she definitely had a thing for a sense of humor.

"Careful. Sounded like you cracked a joke. Wouldn't want to go over the top and make me laugh or anything."

"Is this your idea of flirting?"

"You really don't get out much, do you, Slick?"

"I get out plenty, I just don't meet people like you very often."

"People like me?"

He paused, did that weird piercing eye contact thing again, the same way he'd looked her up and down when he'd come in earlier. This time, her nether regions tingled as if rousing from a long sleep and the way he kept staring at her, homed in on him to give her a wake-up call she'd never forget.

"Forthright. Funny. Interesting."

"So city folk are lying, serious, boring types?"

"Not all. Just the ones I usually meet."

"Well then, you've come to the right place. Love will get under your skin quicker than you think, leaving you wanting more in the end."

A strange expression, part-revulsion, part-fear, flickered across his face though it vanished so quickly she must've imagined it.

"I doubt that. Now, about dinner?"

Nice change of subject. Marc Fairley was uncomfortable with the L word? She'd have to remember that. Playing on a man's weakness was a sure-fire way to bring him to his knees, especially if he got her riled like he had earlier.

"Love Shack it is. The old diner serves a mean burger, the Mexican is authentic and their soda fountain malts are to die for."

He stood, dwarfing her office in an instant. This guy was seriously big and if everything was in proportion...

Stop right there. Don't think GOLF, not in relation to him. Bet he has a lousy swing, a dented club and balls that are skewed.

However, the more she tried not to, the more her mind

drifted south and she struggled for her eyes not to follow suit.

"Soda fountain? You're kidding, right?" Shaking his head, he chuckled. "I've stepped into a time warp and ended up in a rerun of Happy Days."

Before she could respond his intense gaze swept her body, sending a sizzle of heat from her fingertips to her toes, as she wished for a chunk of Kryptonite to stop from melting.

"Though you sure as hell don't look like Joanie. See you there around seven?"

She nodded and he sauntered out the door, leaving her squirming like one of Uncle Hank's worms on the end of a hook.

She tore the Post-it note out of her drawer, screwed it into a tight wad and lobbed it into the trash, muttering "damn golf" and other atrocities as she tried to refocus on work.

After her fourth attempt at analyzing Cupid's latest data matches, Sierra pushed away from her desk and grabbed her bag. Her concentration was shot and she needed a caffeine injection, pronto.

The cappuccino she'd sculled thirty minutes ago didn't have her half as wired as her run-in with City Boy and while another coffee mightn't be the best idea she could do with the walk to Aphrodite's.

She inhaled as she stepped out into the sunshine, calmed by the sweet, heavy scent of freesias in the air. She loved the delicate pink and white flowers tinged with gold, their heady perfume a reminder of the first time she'd set foot in town and been captivated by the abundance of bright flowers in pots along Main Street.

With Dolores hanging onto her hand for fear she'd bolt

she'd been dragged up this street, sullen and silent while her mom grinned at everyone like a newly crowned Miss California greeting fans.

While mom had done the royal wave, Sierra had avoided eye contact and counted pots outside the shopfronts, focusing on the thin stems and delicate petals to curb the rising panic with every step into town.

She'd lost her dad, her hometown, her school, and her friends in the space of a week. Arriving in Love sucked.

Fear had numbed her feet, anesthetized her heart and produced a healthy distrust of males that lingered to this day but Love had grown on her, had become a comfortable fit and every season the freesias bloomed she was reminded how far she'd come from that scared, lost little girl.

She loved Main Street, its eclectic shops a draw for tourists and locals alike. She regularly shopped at the organic grocer, the toffee store and the coffee house, partial to the freshly ground beans from around the world.

Tourists preferred the funky fashions in a string of tiny boutiques stocking everything from kaftans to love beads, loitered in the aromatherapist's and spent a squillion on souvenirs in Amor's Corner Shop.

The town hadn't lost its cozy charm despite the constant influx of rubberneckers and while there were regular complaints about the lack of restaurants and bars, she liked knowing everyone when she headed to Venus for a Margarita or a delish meal at the Love Shack.

She reached the end of the block, turned left past the grade and high schools, crossed the town square and passed the town hall, following her nose and the scent of soul-reviving coffee as she pushed aside a curtain of hanging beads and stepped into Aphrodite, the best café this side of LA.

While the faded linoleum floor, mismatched tables, wobbly chairs and gingham curtains weren't as aesthetically pleasing as a shiny new Starbucks or Gloria Jeans, the coffees were to die for.

"The usual, love?"

Sierra shook her head at Cythera, the owner. While the forty-something woman with a penchant for dreadlocks and crystals denied it, everyone reckoned she'd changed her name to that of a Greek-Cyprian love goddess to fit in with the town's theme.

"I'm in the mood for something different, Cy. Something cold."

"Caffé Freddo?"

"Is that your fancy iced coffee?"

"With an extra dollop of homemade vanilla ice cream on top."

"Done."

Sierra glanced at her watch, remembering the stack of data matches she had to process before knocking off for the day. "Make that to go, please."

"Sure thing."

Cy fiddled with the espresso machine and the aroma of freshly ground coffee beans made Sierra salivate. "How's the dating business these days?"

"Busy."

"You remember my preferences?"

Sierra bit back a grin. Cy regularly interrogated her on likely prospects when she came in for a caffeine fix but Sierra hadn't yet come up with a six-five Nordic god who played the harp, debated philosophy and read tarot.

"I'm keeping my eyes open," Sierra said, sliding her money across the counter as Cy handed over a tall iced coffee. "Promise I'll let you know when the man of your dreams pops up."

"Is that what you told my mother?"

Sierra stiffened, the deep voice perilously close to her ear, her skin prickling exactly like it had earlier when City Boy had strutted into her office.

Damn his soulful, all-night-dirty-talk timbre designed to melt. Like his looks weren't enough.

With Cy riveted to their every word, Sierra forced a sassy smile and turned to face him.

"Sorry, can't disclose that kind of information."

Rather than backing up and giving her room to move, Marc leaned closer, invading her personal space, reinforcing exactly how tall he was.

"What *can* you disclose?"

"Nothing."

"Why am I taking you to dinner then?"

"You're buying? Great. See you then."

She edged around him, only to be halted by an arm that shot out and braced behind her, effectively pinning her between a wall of broad chest and a stainless steel counter.

"Where's the fire?"

Burning her up from the inside out as a startling desire ripped through her, fierce, potent, out of control.

She swallowed and resisted the urge to run her iced coffee across her brow as he smiled. A triumphant smile that said he knew exactly how his nearness affected her and was loving every minute of it, a sexy smile that drew her gaze to the groove in his cheek.

Her hand clenched with the effort not to reach out and touch it, dip her finger in it and by the time she registered the crackle of crumbling Styrofoam, it was too late. He yelped as creamy froth exploded from the top of her take-out cup and sprayed his shirt.

"Oops."

He leaped back and muttered a curse as he grabbed a bunch of serviettes from the counter and dabbed at the mess while she deposited the offending iced coffee on the counter.

The harder she tried not to laugh, the more her mouth twitched and when a few stray milk foam blobs landed on his shiny shoes in the shape of a smiley face, she lost it.

"You're nothing but trouble," he said, resident frown back in place as she howled with laughter, great loud belly laughs that had Cy darting concerned glances their way while serving the other lone customer in the café.

"Sorry," she managed to say between guffaws, swallowing a chuckle, only to find another bubbling up in its place, tickling her throat, irrepressibly infectious.

"If your apology was genuine, I'd accept it. As it is—" he shrugged, dumped the sodden serviettes in the trash reserved for empty sugar packets and stick stirrers, "—you owe me."

"What did you have in mind?"

His heated stare had her wanting to dunk in a vat of iced coffee to cool off.

"I'll think of something."

Oh boy.

"Dinner for starters?"

"Looking forward to it."

She bolted before she told him exactly what kind of payment system she'd like to instigate to make up for her clumsiness.

"Hey. You forgot your coffee."

With her hand on the door, she turned, her gaze sliding

down his drenched shirt. "It's on you—uh, I mean the house."

He laughed as she'd intended and before he tempted her to flirt some more, she made a run for it.

NOT THE MARRYING KIND
Chapter One

Divorce Diva Daily recommends:
Playlist: "I Will Survive" by Gloria Gaynor
Movie: He's Just Not That into You
Cocktail: Slow, Comfortable Screw

Beck Blackwood could kill them.

Every one of those uptight, conservative pricks. Beck's fingers curled into fists as he paced his office, oblivious to the million-dollar view of the Strip. He liked his office perched on the highest floor of the tallest tower in Vegas. King of the world. No other feeling beat it. Apart from sex, but he'd even given up on that while finagling every detail of this deal.

This deal... He stopped in front of his desk and slammed his fist against the prospectus, the pain not registering half as much as having a boardroom of investors hedge around his win- win deal because his company wasn't respectable enough. Translation: he wasn't respectable enough. Damn it, he thought he'd left his past behind.

He'd thought wrong. Didn't matter he rivaled the richest guys in town for penthouse space, property investments, and fast cars. Because of his lifestyle choices—single, heterosexual guy who enjoyed his freedom—and the City of Sin he chose to live in, they didn't deem him worthy. Throw in the PR disaster when his site manager was found in a compromising position with an apprentice on one of his prominent constructions recently, and the fate of Blackwood Enterprises had been sealed.

Vegas loved a scandal. Sex between a married guy and a barely eighteen-year-old girl? The press attacked. Every newspaper article had shown his building site, with his company's name boldly emblazoned with its signature cactus. Damned if the thing didn't add a phallic connotation to every word printed.

Never mind he'd fired the manager and set up counseling for the teenager if she needed it.

Never mind he'd been working his ass off trying to recoup losses the company had sustained in the crash of 2008.

Never mind he'd spent the last eighteen months living and breathing this deal to build hotels across the country that would see company profit margins soar again.

Blackwood Enterprises had been crucified. All his hard work down the toilet because they didn't deem him good enough.

Fuck them. He'd sat in the boardroom after presenting projected statistics that would've had guys with half a brain salivating, rage simmering, as each and every one of the pompous bastards scrambled for excuses.

Too big a risk. People are still talking about your company, and not in a good way.

The face of this project needs to have solid family values. What they were basically saying was that because one of his employees screwed up and he didn't have a band on his ring finger, he wasn't good enough.

Bullshit. His intercom buzzed and he glared at it, not in the mood for interruptions, not in the mood for anything unless it involved eight signatures on the construction deal of a lifetime.

"What is it, Simone?"

"Mr. Robinson wanted to remind you about the function you're planning."

He bit back his first response—*Screw Lou*. "Tell him I'm on it."

"Will do, Mr. Blackwood."

"And I'm incommunicado for the next hour." It'd take him that long to calm down.

"Okay." The intercom fell silent and he flung himself into a chair, ready to tackle a stack of quotes. However, the requisite quick glance at his inbox stalled when he glimpsed an email, every word from Stan Walkerville punctuating his disillusionment at losing out on the deal of the century.

Beck's gut twisted. Stan, the unofficial appointed leader of the investors he'd been counting on earlier today, reiterated his disappointment they wouldn't be building the biggest chain of hotels America had ever seen.

Not half as disappointed as he was. The fortune he'd amassed meant jack if they didn't consider him reliable enough. What did the old farts expect, for him to marry to become the biggest name in construction in the country?

Frigging great, he was back to this. His foolhardy plan. It had first come to him in the meeting when the investors were delivering their verdict because of the tainted Blackwood name. He'd wanted to yell, *What the fuck do you expect me to do, pull a wife out of my ass for respectability?*

While he'd wisely kept his temper in check at the time, the dumb idea had stuck in his head like a burr, no matter how many times he dismissed it. Stupid thing was, he'd analyzed it from every angle and he kept coming back to it.

He needed instant propriety to clear his company's name and get the investors on his side again.

A wife would do that. *Shit.* He re-read the email. Twice. Focused on the last line. *If circumstances change, call us. We'd love to do business.* Was it as simple as that? Get hitched? Become the best in the business? Make his dream of being the biggest in America come true?

Only one problem. Where the hell was he going to find a wife? Hating what an idiot he was for even considering getting married for business, Beck scanned the rest of the emails, eventually finding the one he was searching for.

Late last night he'd agreed to another outlandish idea. Lou Robinson, his Chief Financial Officer and oldest friend, had latched onto a crazy idea to throw a party to celebrate Lou's divorce. Worse, in an effort to get Lou refocused on the job and to ensure word didn't get out his company was promoting divorce—another black mark against it for sure—Beck had said he'd organize it. Anything to snap the usually astute CFO out of his crappy mood.

Besides, organizing some senseless party had to be better than punching the wall. It'd take his mind off the deal long enough for him to come up with a viable solution for Stan and Co. to quit stalling and sign. One that didn't involve shackling himself to a woman. He grimaced at the thought and as the crisp website in fuchsia font came up, he wrinkled his nose.

Divorce Diva Daily. Apart from some nifty alliteration, he had a feeling this site offered nothing but a few party favors at an exorbitant price. Not that he objected to Lou spending a fortune on exorcising his demons. Hell, he'd chip in, no matter how much it took. The faster he threw this party, the faster he could have his competent CFO back.

Beck had an agenda. Schedule a meeting with the probable charlatan running this site, organize the party, make sure Lou was back on the job Monday. To come up with a feasible Plan B to wow the investors, he needed his friend alert and focused, two things he hadn't been able to attribute to Lou in a while. Lou needed to get drunk and get laid. He'd latched onto this lame-ass party idea instead. Whatever. If a divorce party would get Lou back on track, Beck was all for it. The faster he could get this organized and happening, the better.

Against his better judgment, he started reading the diva's blog entry for today.

Top Tips for moving on:

Remove all traces of the ex from your habitat— including corny first-date memorabilia, Valentine's Day cards (commercialistic crap), all engagement and marriage photos, and barf-worthy sentimental gifts.

Beck's mouth quirked at crap and barf. A woman after his own heart.

Smells are powerful reminders. If after several wash cycles his or her stink remains, burn the item involved.

Stink? Beck eased into a smile.

Music is an excellent purging tool. Download the following and crank to full volume:

"You Oughta Know" by Alanis Morrisette

"Survivor" by Destiny's Child

"Harden My Heart" by Quarterflash

"I'm Free" by Rolling Stones

"Goodbye Earl" by Dixie Chicks

Stock up on beverages. Whether hot chocolate or appletinis or Budweisers are your poison, make sure you have plenty. You'll need it for step 5.

Throw the party of the year. Invite your closest friends

and whoop it up. Thank them for supporting you. Forget the past. Move forward.

Let Divorce Diva Daily help you help yourself.

Okay, so the ending lacked the chutzpah of the earlier tips, but he kinda liked this diva. Sure, she was touting a spiel for business, but he could see the appeal in forgetting the past and moving forward.

He'd done a stand-up job of that himself. It was what drove him every day. Making sure he earned enough money and held enough power to ensure he'd never again have to tolerate the condescending, pitiful stares of people looking down on him because he had nothing.

Growing up destitute in Checkerville ensured he'd bottled those feelings of resentment and bitterness. He had used them to great effect studying endlessly to win a scholarship to college, cramming all-nighters to ace tests, and scrimping every cent he earned in part-time jobs to buy land in Vegas just before the boom hit.

Yeah, he'd shown them all. But it was days like today, when the investors stared at him with the same condescension he'd experienced in his youth that old insecurities he thought long buried flared to life. Everyone in Vegas had a past and he'd paid his dues: self-made millionaire who'd grown up tough. He hadn't hid his past from anyone. Which made their rejection now all the more infuriating.

Annoyed at the turn his thoughts were taking, he hit the "About Us" button and scanned for the price list— nada but "Price on Application." He didn't trust POA. Price on Application gave potential shysters free rein. The last thing Lou needed now was to be shafted by a shady online company.

He checked the contact details, coming up with an

email address to a faceless provider. No phone number. No address. Definitely shady.

Like that'd stop him. With a few clicks of his mouse, he'd IM'd a PI who'd done some work for him when hiring prospective employees. Beck didn't like surprises and he didn't trust an anonymous website.

In less than five minutes he had more information. Links between the quirky divorce diva and a party planning company in Provost that had candid testimonials from an extensive list of genuine clientele.

Which made him wonder. Why wouldn't the diva capitalize on the positive PR of an established company? What did she have to hide?

Instincts told him to blow off this diva and find a legit planner, but what if Lou balked and wasted more time? Beck needed a new plan to wow the investors, and that meant having Lou back on board ASAP.

The fastest option would be to follow through with Lou's choice and get this party happening. To do that, he'd have a face-to-face meeting with the diva by the end of the day.

Then he'd focus on more important matters: like finding a quickie wife.

≈

"Sleazy."

"You think?" Poppy Collins stopped scrolling through her iPod for appropriate break-up songs to add to her new blog and glared at her BFF, Ashlee.

"Divorce is painful for a lot of people. And you're making fun of it." Ashlee pointed at the computer screen where Poppy had uploaded her latest post for Divorce Diva

Daily, the blog that would single-handedly save Party Hard, her sister's party planning business.

"I'm intending on making a lot of money from it," Poppy muttered, tossing her iPod on the desk and swinging her chair to face Ashlee. "Money that's going to keep you employed."

Ashlee winced. "Financials that bad?"

"You're Sara's assistant. You tell me." Poppy hated seeing her driven, career-oriented sister in a deep depression that had almost cost her the business. She hated seeing Sara's smug, WASP ex Wayne, prancing around town in a midlife-crisis-red convertible more.

Suburban Provost on the outskirts of Los Angeles wasn't big enough for both of them, which was why Poppy had insisted that Sara recuperate at a private clinic in LA while Poppy put her freelance promotion business on hold, utilized her marketing degree, and ran the business.

Problem was, Poppy knew as much about party planning as she did about relationships: absolutely zilch.

The divorce party idea was her last stand. It had to work. Sara had lost Wayne the Pain. No way would Poppy let her lose her prized business, too. It was all Sara had left.

"But celebrating divorce is tacky," Ashlee said, her gaze drawn to the PC screen again. "We'll get crucified by every do-gooder along the western seaboard."

"That's why Divorce Diva is anonymous. Plus Sara would throw a hissy fit over the D-word, so best to keep this under the radar." Poppy tapped her temple. "Up here for thinking." She pointed at her favorite crimson pumps with the three-inch stiletto heels covered in sparkles. "Down there for dancing."

"Planning parties online is one thing. What if someone wants a one-on-one consult?" Ashlee's frown deepened.

"You're not a party planner. You're a party pooper." Poppy blew out a long breath. "One step at a time, okay?"

"I've got a bad feeling about this."

"And I've got a worse one about this." Poppy stabbed at the stack of bills teetering next to her in-tray. "This idea doesn't take off? We're history."

And Sara would lose everything. No way would she let that happen. She owed her sister. Big time.

Ashlee made disapproving clicking noises. "But divorce is so...so..."

"Inevitable? Guaranteed? Worth celebrating?"

"Private. Painful. Devastating."

"And that's exactly why I'm doing this."

Poppy had seen what impending divorce had done to Sara. Her vibrant, career-driven sis had fallen apart when Wayne walked out, and she'd been a zombie for months, popping anti-depressants until Poppy organized a prolonged stay at the clinic, complete with on-site psychologists. Sara had made progress, but to see her listless without an ounce of spark rammed home for Poppy the fact that love came with risks. Big ones.

Despite the best medical supervision, counseling, and medication, Sara languished, rehashing every reason why her marriage had failed. Poppy could've saved her a fortune in therapy bills with the truth: Wayne was an immature asshole who'd spend his life and fortune searching for the next best thing. Guys like him were never happy with what they had for long. They grew bored. They needed shiny new toys. They kept looking for something bigger and better. Splashing their cash around, seeking vicarious thrills...but they were never truly happy. Narcissistic jerks.

When Sara was ready, Poppy would help her move on with the biggest damned divorce party she could throw.

Until then, it was imperative she kept Divorce Diva a secret from her stressed-out sis. With Sara's divorce imminent, no way would she approve, and Poppy didn't want her idea scuttled before it had a chance to work. Or worse, cause a relapse when Sara had finally begun to make progress.

Poppy would do whatever it took to save Sara's business. Plenty of time later to clue Sara in—after she'd succeeded.

"Divorce parties are all about marking the end of suffering and starting fresh. We have rituals for everything else—weddings, births, deaths—why not divorce?"

Ashlee said nothing, her compressed lips and dent between her brows conveying her disapproval.

"A new phase in life is worth celebrating." Damned straight she'd help Sara celebrate The Pain's exit. But if Ashlee didn't buy the professional spiel Poppy had concocted, prospective clients wouldn't either and that would signal the end. "Plus it can be an opportunity for the newly single to thank all the people who've stood by him or her during the ordeal."

Another thing that had torn Sara apart was losing so many of her friends, those tiresome couples who were happy to hang out with other married peeps but scattered when the couple split. What was up with that? Like friendships were expendable or based on the glittery bauble on your ring finger?

"Friends can throw a party to show their divorcing pal they're supported and not alone. Or it can be a time to vent, cry, yell, laugh, whatever, in the company of people who love you." Sara had done enough crying. Poppy would ensure she whooped it up at her divorce party. "What's so bad about that?"

"I still say it's tacky." Starry-eyed, recently engaged Ashlee would think anything tarnishing the holy sanctity of marriage was tacky. Wait until dearly beloved Craig started working nights and taking longer interstate trips and deleting text messages as soon as they pinged. Then she'd get a reality check.

"We're not promoting divorce. We're giving people the option to celebrate it once it's final." Poppy pushed a stack of literature across the desk toward Ashlee. "I've researched this thoroughly. Divorce parties are the latest and greatest. Party planners are raking it in. We have to do this—it's good business."

"I guess." Ashlee gnawed her bottom lip and darted a nervous glance at the stack of bills.

"No guesswork. Divorce Diva Daily is going to rock." Feigning confidence, Poppy interlocked her hands behind her head and leaned back.

"It better. Or we'll be back serving ice creams at Iggy's." Ashlee made a mock gagging motion and Poppy wrinkled her nose at memories of their first job in high school. Iggy had a thing for cones—of every variety—and often rocked up to the shop stoned out of his head, sharing the love by feeling up his employees and giving away freebies. The only reason he was still in business was customer loyalty. Provost looked after its own. Poppy hoped that kind of loyalty extended to Party Hard if her Divorce Diva Daily idea went belly-up and Sara lost everything.

"It'll work, trust me."

Ashlee perched on the desk. "Like how I trusted you with my mom's bachelorette party and we almost landed in jail?" She held up her fingers and started counting off misdemeanors. "Like how I trusted you with my secret make-out place and the entire tenth grade ended up there? Like—"

"Build a bridge, hon." Poppy grinned and waved away

Ashlee's concerns, thankful her best friend was along for a ride that promised to be bumpy at best.

A smile tugged at the corners of Ashlee's mouth. "I'll get over it when you prove you've matured beyond high school."

"Hey, I'm mature."

Ashlee raised an imperious eyebrow and pointed at her desk. "You're saving a printed RPatz autographed Twilight flyer, your Gryffindor Forever stick-on tattoos are plastered everywhere, and you've been clubbing three times this week."

"I like to bust a move."

"And the rest?"

"Can never have enough sparkly vamps or Harry Potter around."

"Just make this work, okay?" Ashlee's reluctant smile turned into a full-fledged grin as she tapped the stack of bills with a magenta-tipped fingernail.

"You bet." Poppy saluted. It wasn't until Ashlee bustled out of her office that Poppy slumped in her seat, glaring at the bills like they were radioactive.

No matter how many times Divorce Diva Daily recommended songs like Stevie Nicks's "Stop Dragging Your Heart Around" or ELO's "Don't Bring Me Down," they needed parties to plan.

First request that came in? She'd bust her ass making it the best damned divorce party ever.

No problemo.

FAKING IT
Chapter One

Look up *stupid* in the dictionary and you'll find my picture.

Along with revealing stats: Shari Jones, twenty-nine, five-seven, black hair, hazel eyes, New Yorker. Addicted to toxic men like my ex, cheesecake, and mojitos (not necessarily in that order), and willing to do anything for a friend, including travel to India and impersonate aforementioned friend in an outlandish plot to ditch her fiancé.

See? Stupid.

"You're the best." Amrita Muthu, my zany best friend who devised this escapade, cut a wedge of chocolate cheesecake and plopped it on my plate. "Have another piece to celebrate."

I loved how she always had cheesecake stocked in her apartment freezer but as I stared at my favorite dessert I knew I couldn't afford the extra calories. Not with my destination of Mumbai—land of food hospitality—where I'd be bombarded with rich, sugar-laden treats that I'd have to eat to be polite.

Despite my Indo-American heritage, *jalebis, gulab jamuns*, and *rasmalai* are not my idea of heaven. The sickly sweet morsels were a testament to years as a fat kid, courtesy of an Indian mother who wasn't satisfied until my eyes —as well as my waistline—were bulging from too much food.

"Eat up, my girl," Mom used to say, shoveling another mini Mount Everest of rice and *dahl* onto my plate. "Lentils are strengthening. They'll make you big and strong."

She'd been right about the big part. Still waiting for my muscles to kick in.

But hey, I survived the food fest, and thanks to hours in the gym, smaller portions of *dahl* (yeah, I'd actually become hooked on the stuff), and moving away from home, I now had a shape that didn't resemble a blimp.

"Shari? You going to eat or meditate?"

"Shut up." I glared at Amrita—Rita to me—then picked up my fork and toyed with the cheesecake. "Too early for celebrations." *Commiserations* were more likely if this wacky plot imploded. "You're not the one spending two weeks in Mumbai with a bunch of strangers, pretending to like them."

"But you don't have to pretend. That's the whole point. I want you to be yourself and convince the Ramas I'm not worthy of their son." Rita stuck two fingers down her throat and made gagging noises. "Bet he's a real prince. Probably expects the prospective good little Hindu wife he's never seen to bow, kiss his ass, and bear him a dozen brats. Like that's going to happen."

She rolled her perfectly kohled eyes and cut herself another generous slab of cheesecake. Curves are revered in India and Rita does her heritage proud with an enviable hourglass figure.

"You think my naturally obnoxious personality will drive this prince away, huh? Nice."

Rita grinned and topped off our glasses from the mojito pitcher sitting half-empty between us. "You know what I mean. You're flamboyant, assertive, eloquent. Except when it came to your ex." She made a thumbs-down sign. "I'm a wimp when it comes to defying my folks. If anyone can get me out of this mess, you can."

Debatable, considering the mess I'd made of my life lately.

"No way would I marry some stooge and leave NYC to live in Mumbai. Not happening."

She took a healthy slurp of mojito and ran a crimson-tipped fingernail around the rim of the glass. "Besides, you score a free trip. Not to mention the added bonus of putting Tate behind you once and for all."

That did it. I pushed my plate away and sculled my mojito. The mention of Tate Embley, my ex-boyfriend, ex-landlord, and ex-boss turned my stomach. Rita was right—I *was* assertive, which made what happened with him all the more unpalatable. I'd been a fool, falling for a slick, suave lawyer who'd courted me with a practiced flair I'd found lacking in the guys I'd dated previously.

I'd succumbed to the romance, the glamour, the thrill. Tate had been attentive and complimentary and generous. And I'd tumbled headfirst into love, making the fact he'd played me from start to finish harder to accept. Maybe I'd been naïve to believe his lavish promises. Maybe I should've known if something's too good to be true it usually is. Maybe I'd been smitten at the time, blinded to the reality of the situation: an unscrupulous jerk had charmed me into believing his lies to the point I'd lowered my streetwise defenses and toppled into an ill-fated relationship from the beginning.

"Oops, I forgot." Rita's hand flew to her mouth, a mischievous glint in her black eyes. "Wasn't supposed to mention the T-word."

I smirked. "Bitch."

"It's therapeutic to talk about it."

Morose, I stared into my empty glass, knowing a stint in India couldn't be as bad as this. If there's one thing I hate, it's rehashing the mess I'd made of my love life. "What's there to talk about? We're over."

"Over, schmover. If he came groveling on his Armani knees you'd reconsider." She jabbed a finger at me. "If he comes sniffing aroundyou again I'll kick his sorry ass to the curb."

"I already tried kicking him to the curb and now I'm homeless and unemployed."

Three months later, I couldn't believe he'd played me, thrown me out of his swank Park Avenue apartment, and fired me all on the same day. So what if I'd called him a lying, sleazy bastard with the morals of a rabid alley cat? If the Gucci loafer fit...

Rita refilled my glass, her stern glare nothing I hadn't seen before. "He'd reduced you to ho status. He paid your salary, your rent, and left you the odd tip when he felt like it."

She stared at the princess-cut ruby edged in beveled diamonds on the third finger of my right hand and I blushed, remembering the exact moment Tate had slipped it on. We'd been holed up in his apartment for a long weekend and in the midst of our sex-a-thon he'd given me the ring. Maybe I'd felt like Julia Roberts getting a bonus from Richard Gere for all of two seconds, but hey, it'd been different. I loved the guy. He loved me.

Yeah, right.

Tate had strung me along for a year, feeding me all the right lines: his wife didn't love him, platonic marriage, they never had sex, they stayed together for appearances, he'd leave her soon, blah, blah, blah.

Stupidly, I believed him until that fateful day three months ago when someone at Embley Associates, one of New York's premier law firms, revealed the latest juicy snippet: Tate, the firm's founding partner, was going to be a daddy. After years of trying with his gorgeous wife, nudge, nudge, wink, wink.

Say no more.

Unfortunately, Tate had tried some schmoozy winking with me to gloss over his *I was drunk, she took advantage of me, it won't change a thing between us* spiel. I'd nudged him right where it hurt and things had spiraled downhill from there.

Hence, my homeless, unemployed, and dumped status.

I folded my arms to hide the offending bauble—which was so damn pretty I couldn't part with it despite being tempted to pay rent. "Your point?"

"Forget him. Forget your problems. Go to India, live it up."

"And save your ass in the process?"

Rita grinned and clinked glasses with mine. "Now you're on the right track."

"I must be crazy."

"Or desperate."

"That, too." I shook my head. "Have you really thought this through? Word travels fast in your family."

"We've been planning this for a month. It'll work." Rita lowered her glass, an uncharacteristic frown slashing her brows. "You've been living here. You've seen my mom in action. You know why I have to do this."

She had a point. While every aspect of Rita's Hinduism fascinated an atheist like me, her double life was exhausting. Her folks would be scandalized if they knew she drank alcohol and ate beef, forbidden in her religion. But according to my inventive friend, who liked to stretch boundaries, cows in New York weren't holy and the alcohol helped her assimilate. Likely excuses, but living beneath the burden of her family's expectations—including an arranged marriage to a guy halfway around the world—had taken its toll. She needed to tell her folks the truth, but for now she'd settled on this crazy scheme to buy herself time to build up the courage.

I could've persuaded her to come clean, but I went along with it because I owed Rita. Big-time. She'd let me crash here, she'd listened to my sob story repeatedly, she'd waived rent while I fruitlessly job-searched. Apparently out-of-work legal secretaries were as common in job interviews as rats were in the subway. Didn't help that the low-key, detail-oriented job bored me to tears in my last year at Embley Associates, and I'd been wistfully contemplating a change. Therein lay the problem. I needed to work for living expenses and bills and rent but my personal fulfillment well was dry and in serious need of a refill.

Another reason I was doing this: I hoped traveling to Mumbai would give me a fresh perspective. Besides, I could always add actress/ impersonator to my résumé to jazz it up when I returned.

"Telling your family would be easier." On both of us, especially me, the main stooge about to perpetuate this insanity. "What if I mess up? It'll be a disaster."

Oblivious to my increasing nerves, Rita's frown cleared. "It'll be a cinch. My aunt Anjali's in on the plan, and she'll meet you at the airport and guide you through the Rama rigmarole. She's a riot and you'll love staying with her. Consider it a well-earned vacation." She clicked her fingers and grinned. "A vacation that includes giving the Ramas' dweeby son the cold shoulder so he can't stand the thought of marrying me. Capish?"

"Uh-huh."

Could I really pull this off? Posing as an arranged fiancée, using a smattering of my rusty Hindi, immersing in a culture I hadn't been a part of since my family had moved to the States when I was three. Though I was half Indian, spending the bulk of my life in New York had erased my childhood memories of the exotic continent that held little fascination for me. Sure, Mom told stories about her homeland and continued to whip up Indian feasts that would do a maharajah proud, yet it all seemed so remote, so distant.

It hadn't been until I'd become friends with Rita, who worked at Bergdorf's in accounts—and who gave me a healthy discount once we'd established a friendship—that my latent interest in my heritage had been reawakened.

Rita had intrigued me from the start, her sultry beauty, her pride in her culture, her lilting singsong accent. She encapsulated everything Indian, and though my life had temporarily fallen apart thanks to the Toad—my penchant for nicknames resonated in this instance, considering Tate was cold and slimy—the opportunity to travel to India and help Rita in the process had been too tempting to refuse.

"You sure this Rakesh guy doesn't know what you look like?"

"I'm sure." Her smug smile didn't reassure me. "I'm not on Facebook and I Googled myself three times to make sure there were no pics. You'll be pleased to know I'm decidedly un-Google-worthy. As for the photo my parents sent before they left... well, let's just say there was a little problem in transit."

"Tell me you didn't interfere with the U.S. Postal Service."

"'Course not." Her grin widened. "I tampered with the Muthu Postal Service."

"Which means?"

"Mom gave Dad a stack of mail to send. He was giving me a ride, and when he stopped to pick up his favorite tamarind chutney I pilfered the envelope out of the bunch."

"Slick."

"I think so." She blew on her nails and polished them against her top, her 'I'm beyond cool' action making me laugh. "Besides, we look enough alike that even if he caught a sneak peek at some photo, it shouldn't be a problem."

Luckily, I had cosmopolitan features that could pass for any number of backgrounds: Spanish, Italian, Portuguese, or Mexican. Few people pegged me for half Indian, not that I'd played it down or anything. In a country as diverse as the U.S., an exotic appearance was as common as a Starbucks on every corner.

"I like your confidence," I said, my droll response garnering a shrug.

"You'll be fine."

"Easy for you to say." I twirled the stem of my cocktail glass, increasingly edgy. "Even if this works, won't your folks fix you up with another guy?"

"Leave my parents' future matchmaking propositions to me." She snapped her fingers, her self-assurance admirable. "If they try this again, I'll pull the 'I'm your only child and you'll never see me again' trick. That'll scare them. I would've done it now but they've planned this Grand Canyon trip for a decade and I would've hated seeing them cancel it, and lose a small fortune, over me."

She paused, tapped her bottom lip, thinking, as I inwardly shuddered at what she'd come up with next. "Though I do feel sorry for them, what with Anjali being their only living relative, which is why I pretended to go along with this farce of marrying Rakesh in the first place."

"You're all heart."

She punched me lightly on the upper arm. "You can do this."

"I guess." My lack of enthusiasm elicited a frown.

"Here's the info dossier. Keep it safe."

She handed me a slim manila folder, the beige blandly discreet.

Welcome to my life as a 007 sidekick. Halle Berry? Nah, I'm not that vain. Miss Moneypenny? Not that old, though considering the time I'd wasted on Tate, I was starting to feel it.

"My future as a single woman able to make her own life choices depends on it."

I rolled my eyes but took the folder. "I know everything there is to know about the Rama family. You've drilled me for a month straight."

"Okay, wiseass. Who's the father and what does he do?"

I sipped at my mojito and cleared my throat, trying not to chuckle at Rita's obvious impatience as she drummed her fingernails against the armrest. "Too easy. Senthil Rama, musician, plays tabla for Bollywood movies."

"The mother?"

"Anu. Bossy cow."

A smile tugged at the corners of Rita's crimson-glossed mouth.

"Sisters?"

"Three. Pooja, Divya, and Shruti. Watch them. If the mom's a cow, they're the calves." Rita's smile turned into a full-fledged grin. "And last but not least?"

"Rakesh Rama. Betrothed to Amrita Muthu, New York City girl shirking her familial responsibility, besmirching her Hindu heritage, shaming her mother, disappointing her father, embroiling her best friend in deception—"

"Smartass."

Rita threw a silk-covered cushion at my head, and thanks to the four mojitos I'd consumed my reaction time slowed and it hit me right between the eyes. Reminiscent of the lapis lazuli paperweight I'd thrown at Tate as I slammed out of his office that last time. Pity my aim wasn't as good as Rita's.

Her scheme might be crazy but I knew I was doing the right thing. India would buy me some thinking time about what I wanted to do with my life.

I dribbled the last precious drops from the mojito jug into our glasses and raised mine in Rita's direction. "To Bollywood and back. Bottoms up."

~

"Oh. My. *God*."

Shielding my eyes from the scorching glare of Mumbai's midday sun, I ran across the tarmac like a novice on hot coals, seeking shade in the terminal yet terrified by the sea of faces confronting me. How many people were meeting this flight?

A guy jostled me as I neared the terminal, my filthy glare wasted when he patted my arm, mumbled an apology, and slid into the crowd. I wouldn't have given the incident a second thought if not for the way his hand had lingered on my arm, almost possessively. Creep.

I picked up the pace, ignoring the stares prickling between my shoulder blades. Were the hordes ogling me, or was that my latent paranoia flaring already? *There's the imposter—expose her*.

I battled customs and fought my way through the seething mass of humanity to grab my luggage from the carousel. Caught up in a surge toward the arrival hall, *culture shock* took on new meaning as men, women, and children screeched and waved and hugged. On the outskirts I spotted a woman holding aloft a miniature Statue of Liberty, like Buffy brandishing a cross to ward off the vamps.

I'd laughed when Rita told me what her aunt would use

to identify herself at Mumbai airport; now that I'd been smothered by a blanket of heat and aromas I didn't dare identify, jostled by pointy elbows, and sweated until my peasant top clung to my back, it wasn't so funny.

I used my case as a battering ram as I pushed through the crowd toward the Statue of Liberty. I'd never been so relieved to see that lovely Lady and her spiked halo.

"*Namaste*, Auntie," I said, unsure whether to press my palms together in the traditional Hindi greeting with a slight bow, hug her, or reel back from the garlic odor clinging to her voluminous cobalt sari.

She took the dilemma out of my hands by dropping the statue into her bag and wrapping her arms around me in a bear hug. "Shari, my child. Welcome. We talk English, yes?"

Holding my breath against the garlic fumes, I managed a nod as she pulled away and held me at arm's length.

"That naughty girl Amrita didn't tell me how beautiful you are. Why aren't you married?"

Great. I'd escaped my mom's Gestapo-like interrogations only to have Anjali pick up the slack. I mumbled something indecipherable, like 'mind your own business,' and smiled demurely. No use alienating the one woman who was my ally for the next two weeks.

"Never mind. Once this Rama rubbish is taken care of, maybe you'll fall in love with a nice Indian boy, yes?" Anjali cocked her head to one side, her beady black eyes taking on a decidedly matchmaking gleam.

I don't think so! I thought.

"Pleasure to meet you, Auntie," I said.

Rather than quiz me about my lack of marriage prospects she beamed, tucked her arm through mine, and dragged me toward the exit where another throng waited to get in. "Come, I have a car waiting. You must be exhausted after your flight. A good cup of *chai* and a few *ladoos* will revive you."

Uh-oh. The sweet-stuffing tradition had begun. *Ladoos* were lentil-laden balls packed with *ghee*, Indian clarified butter designed to add a few fat rolls in that fleshy gap between the sari and the *choli*, the short top worn beneath. Mom's favorite was *besan ladoos* and I remembered their smooth, nutty texture melting in my mouth. Despite my vow to stay clear of the sweets, saliva pooled and I swallowed, hoping I could resist.

Exiting the terminal equated with walking into a furnace and I dabbed at the perspiration beading on my top lip as Anjali signaled to a battered Beamer. "My driver will have us home shortly."

I didn't care if her driver beamed me up to the moon, as long as the car had air-conditioning.

While Anjali maintained a steady stream of conversation on the way to her house, I developed a mild case of whiplash as my head snapped every which way, taking in the sights of downtown Mumbai.

Cars, diesel-streaming buses, motorbikes, bicycles, and auto-rickshaws battled with a swarming horde of people on the clogged roads in a frightening free-for-all where it was every man, woman, and rickshaw driver for themselves.

The subway on a bad day had nothing on this.

Anjali—immune to the near-death experiences occurring before our eyes—prattled on about *parathas*, my favorite whole-meal flatbread, and her Punjabi neighbors, while I gripped the closest door handle until my fingers ached. Our driver, Buddy (Anjali had had a thing for Buddy Holly and thus dubbed her man-about-the-house Buddy, thanks to his Coke-bottle glasses), maintained a steady stream of Hindi abuse—at least I assumed it was abuse, judging by his volume and hand actions—while his other hand remained planted on the horn.

Pity I hadn't held onto those earplugs from the flight. Would've been handy to mute the Mumbai melodies. I squeezed my eyes shut for the hundredth time as a small child darted out after a mangy dog right in front of our car. On the upside, every time I reopened my eyes, something new captured my attention. Fresh flowers on street corners, roadside vendors frying snacks in giant woks, long, orderly lines at bus stops. Bustling markets and sprawling malls nestled between ancient monuments.

Amazing contrasts—boutiques and five-star restaurants alongside abject poverty, beggars sharing the sidewalks with immaculately coiffed women who belonged on the cover of *Elle*, smog-filled streets while the Arabian Sea stretched as far as the eye could see on the city's doorstep.

When Buddy slowed and turned into a tiny driveway squeezed between a row of faded whitewashed flats, I almost missed the frenetic Mumbai energy that held me enthralled already.

"We're home." Anjali clapped her hands. "Leave your luggage to Buddy. Time to eat."

As I followed Anjali into the blessed coolness of her house, my hands shaking from the adrenaline surging through my system, I had an idea. Maybe soaking *ladoos* in white rum and lime juice would counteract the calories?

My very own Mumbai Mojitos.

Take a bite, get happy.

Eat two, get ecstatic.

Eat a dozen, get catatonic and forget every stupid reason why I'd traveled thousands of miles to pretend to be someone else.

Great, perpetuating this scheme had affected my sense of humor, along with my perspective.

Hoping my duty-free liquor had survived the road trip from hell, I perked up at the thought of my favorite drink (to be consumed on the sly as Rita reminded me a hundred times, in case I forgot I wasn't supposed to drink while impersonating her) and climbed the stairs behind Anjali, trying not to focus on her cracked heels or the silk sari straining over her ample ass.

"Hurry up, child. The *ayah* has outdone herself in preparing a welcome meal for you."

Wishing I had a housemaid-cum-cook back home, I fixed a polite smile on my face as Anjali launched into another nonstop monologue, this time about the joys of grinding spices on a stone over store-bought curry powders. While she chatted I surreptitiously loosened the top button on my jeans in preparation for my initiation into India's national pastime—after cricket, that is.

"I hope you enjoy your curries hot, Shari. Nothing like chili to put pep in your step." Anjali bustled me into a dining room featuring a table covered with enough food to feed the multitudes I'd seen teaming the streets earlier. "Eat up, child. Men like some flesh on their women. Perhaps that's your problem?"

With an ear-jarring cackle, she proceeded to show me exactly how attractive men must find her by heaping a plate with rice, Goan fish curry rich in spices and coconut milk, *baigan aloo* (eggplant and potato), *chana dahl* (lentils), *pappadums* (deep-fried, wafer-thin lentil flour accompaniments resembling giant crisps), and raita (a delicious yoghurt chutney).

Had she noticed I hadn't said more than two words since I arrived? If so, she didn't let on, happily maintaining a steady flow of conversation while making a sizeable dent in the food laid out before us. With constant urging, I managed to eat a reasonable portion of rice and curry, leaving room for the inevitable barrage of sweets, wondering if I could sneak up to my room for a fortifying rum.

However, like most of my dreams in this world, it wasn't to be.

"Excuse me, Missy." Buddy shuffled into the room, his dusty bare feet leaving faint footprints on the polished white tiles. "There's been an accident."

Rather than looking at Anjali, Buddy darted glances at me with frightened doe eyes.

"Spit it out, man. What's happened?" Anjali spoiled her attempt at playing the imperious master standing over her servant by stuffing another ball of rice into her mouth with her curry-covered fingers and smacking her lips.

Buddy stared at me, panic-stricken. "It's the missy's bottles. They broke. Leak everywhere."

"Bottles? What bottles?" Anjali paused mid-chew, her plucked eyebrows shooting skyward.

I rarely swore. In fact, the F-word made me cringe. However, with my stomach rebelling against the onslaught of food, my nerves shot by the drive here, and my secret duty-free mojito stash now in ruins, all I could think was *fuuuuuck*.

~

I wanted to sleep in the next morning but Anjali didn't believe in jet lag. She believed in breakfast at the crack of dawn.

"Eat more, my girl. *Idlis* will give you strength for the day ahead."

She pushed the tray of steamed rice cakes toward me along with the *sambhar*, a lentil soup thick with vegetables.

Not wanting to appear impolite on my first morning here, I spooned another *idli* onto my plate and ladled a sparrow's serving of *sambhar* over it. "What's on for today?"

"I've planned a grand tour of Mumbai especially for you." She held up a hand, fingers extended. "First stop, the Gateway of India."

One finger bent.

"Second, a boat cruise on the harbor."

Another finger lowered.

"Third, Chhatrapati Shivaji Terminus. Then Mani Bhavan, at the home of Mahatma Ghandi."

She waved her pinkie and I hoped our last stop included shopping. "And finally, we eat at my favorite restaurant."

The thought of more food turned the *idlis* to lead in my stomach, and I edged my plate away. She didn't notice, her face glowing with pride, like a kid who nailed a test. I didn't have the heart to tell her I was more interested in Mumbai's malls than cultural icons.

"Sounds good." I injected enthusiasm into my voice, but it wasn't enough to distract Anjali as she eyed my plate and untouched *idli* with a frown.

Thankfully, Buddy entered the dining room and Anjali clapped her hands. "Time to go."

Relieved, I followed her to the car, thanking Buddy for holding open my door as I slid onto the back seat. He shuffled his feet in embarrassment but I caught the flicker of a bashful smile before he slipped behind the steering wheel. He'd been mortified over the duty-free bottle breakage, but what could I do? Confess to a secret alcohol stash? I'd brushed over the incident last night, citing special clear coconut juice I'd brought from the States before hiding the broken glass and condemning labels deeply in the trash. That's all I needed, for some nosy neighbor to out Anjali for secretly swigging alcohol.

As Buddy tested his Angry Birds skills—people were like the game app birds, seemingly flinging themselves at our car—I swallowed a curse. Oblivious to my morbid fear of inadvertently killing one of the many pedestrians jamming the sidewalks and spilling onto the road, Anjali stared at my hands, where I clutched at the worn leather.

"That's a lovely ring." She pointed at the ruby. "From someone special?"

"No." I released my grip on the seat to twist the ring around, wishing I didn't love it so much. Definitely not from someone special.

She didn't probe, her curiosity snagged by my watch. The gold link and diamond TAG had been a gift to myself with my first paycheck at Tate's law firm, a splurge I'd justified at the time by saying I needed to look the part at an upmarket practice, when in reality I'd wanted to impress the boss who'd already made a pass at me during the first two weeks.

"That a gift, too?"

Jeez, who was she, the jewelry police?

"A gift to myself."

Needing a change of topic fast, I pointed out the window. "That's the third cinema we've passed in a few blocks."

She craned her neck for a better look. "Nothing unusual. We're the movie capital of India, so there's a multiplex cinema on every street." She had to be exaggerating, but as Buddy weaved in and out of the road chaos, I spotted five more.

"Personally, I prefer cable." Anjali rummaged around in her giant handbag and pulled out a *TV Soap* magazine. "Hundreds of channels, better viewing."

She flicked it open to a double-page spread of buffed guys with bare chests and brooding expressions. Not bad, if you liked that fake chiseled look. By the twinkle in Anjali's eye as she shoved the magazine my way, she did. "Bill Spencer is my favorite."

Clueless, I shrugged.

Horrified, she stabbed at a photo of a dark-haired, dark-eyed Adonis with rippling pecs and a serious six-pack. "Don Diamont. You've never heard of him? *The Young and the Restless?* Dollar Bill Spencer in *Bold and the Beautiful*?"

"Uh, no, I'm more of a rom-com gal."

Shaking her head, she snapped the magazine shut and thrust it into her bag, casting me a disbelieving glare. "I'm thinking Amrita did you a favor sending you here."

I didn't want to ask, but there was something cutesy and lovable about Anjali, and I couldn't resist. "Why, Auntie?"

"So I can educate you."

I stifled a snort. "About soap operas?"

"About *men*." She rattled her bag for emphasis. "These are the men you must aspire to. Handsome, tall, broad shoulders, rich."

"Fictional," I muttered, earning a click of her tongue.

She crossed her arms, hugging the bag and magazine to her chest.

"You'll see. Once you ditch Anu's son, we can concentrate on finding you another boy."

I refrained from adding, "I want a *man*." No point encouraging her.

Buddy swerved into a narrow parking space between a cart and an auto-rickshaw. I didn't know what was worse:

the promise of Anjali's matchmaking me with a soap-idol lookalike or the ensured whiplash every time I sat in a car.

"Good, we're here." She gathered the folds of her sari like a queen as she stepped from the car. "Where every tourist to Mumbai starts exploring." She threw her arms wide. "The Gateway of India."

I might not be a cultural chick but I had to admit the huge archway on the water's edge was impressive. Roughly sixty feet, it had four turrets and intricate latticework carved into the yellow stone. "What's this made from?"

"Basalt stone, very strong." Anjali linked her elbow through mine and drew me down the steps behind the arch to the water's edge. "Come, we'll take a short cruise on a motor launch."

I eyed the small, bobbing boats dubiously, hoping the captains steered more sedately than the drivers on the roads.

Anjali didn't give me a chance to refuse, slipping a launch operator some rupees and hustling me into a boat before I could feign seasickness. The motor launch shot off at a great speed and I clung onto the seat. Good thing I'd skipped the manicure before I met the Ramas. It'd be shredded by the end of today.

Anjali hadn't prepped me for the upcoming Rama meeting. Not to worry. Rita had more than made up for it. "The Rama welcoming party should be interesting."

"Coming face to face with Rakesh might be interesting." Anjali screwed up her nose. "Meeting that witch Anu?" She muttered a stream of Hindi, her tone vitriolic.

Witch? Intrigued, I waited for a pause. "So you know Anu?"

"You could say that." She folded her arms, her expression thunderous.

O-kay. Untold saga alert. Surprising Rita hadn't

mentioned any history between her aunt and prospective mother-in-law. "Is there a problem between you—"

"Look." Anjali nudged me with her elbow and gestured toward the arch. Nice change of topic.

I conceded for now. "You were right—the view from here is fantastic."

The corners of her eyes crinkled with pride, as if she'd constructed the archway by hand. "It was built to commemorate the first-ever visit by a British monarch, King George V and Queen Mary in 1911."

"Interesting." She was distracting me with a tour guide spiel. I'd play along, lulling her into a false sense of security before resuming my interrogation. I pointed at a beautiful white-turreted, pink-domed building behind the arch. "What's that?"

"The Taj Mahal Palace." She touched the tip of her nose and raised it. "Very posh hotel."

"Maybe Rakesh will take me there?"

"Probably, if he's anything like his bragging mother." Anjali snorted. "I wouldn't know, I haven't been invited to the house yet to meet him, despite being the aunt of his betrothed." She made a disgusted clicking sound with her tongue. "Bet that's Anu's doing, too."

Fascinated by her obvious dislike for Rakesh's mom, I probed further.

"Hope she won't have to chaperone." I subtly sided with Anjali, hoping she'd elaborate.

Her lips thinned. "Don't worry about Anu. I'll deal with her; you take care of breaking the betrothal."

I scrutinized her, mulling her blatant antagonism. Why would a woman who'd been raised to accept arranged marriages be hell-bent on ruining one?

"Why are you helping Rita break her arrangement?"

Startled, Anjali shifted and the boat tipped alarmingly before righting. "Amrita is like a daughter to me. She deserves to choose her happiness."

Deep.

"Not all of us are so lucky." Anjali shrugged, the sadness tightening her mouth, making me wish I hadn't probed.

"What about Senthil? What's he like?" I hoped switching from marriage back to the Ramas would divert her attention.

"Very fine musician." Her lips clamped into a thin, unimpressed line before she turned away.

Guess discussing the Ramas hit a sore spot.

I pointed at a nearby island. "Is that temple significant?"

While Anjali prattled on about nearby Elephanta Island where the Temple Cave of Lord Shiva could be found, I pondered her revelations. She knew next to nothing about Rakesh, admired Senthil's musical skills, and despised Anu. It shouldn't have mattered, but her dislike for Rakesh's mom made me uneasy. If Anjali had another agenda, one I knew nothing about, it could jeopardize our entire scheme. Like I wasn't anxious enough.

I focused on the Mumbai skyline, captured by the complexity of this cosmopolitan city. I'd been here a day and barely scratched the surface, but from what I'd seen on Anjali's grand tour so far I was starting to get a feel for the place.

"You're awfully quiet," Anjali said as the boat docked and I helped her step onto land.

"Just taking it all in." The sights, and the mysterious disclosures.

She patted my arm. "Don't worry about meeting the Ramas. If Rakesh is anything like his father, you'll be fine."

"What's Senthil like?"

"Nice enough." She shrugged, her blasé response belied by a quick look-away.

"Shame I'll be dealing more with Anu and not him."

Anjali frowned. "Be careful with her. She's astute and devious." She made a slitting sign across her throat. "Cunning as a rat. Dangerous when confronted."

Uh-oh. The last thing I needed: a perceptive psycho. My nervousness morphed into full-blown terror.

Before I could discover more, Buddy pulled up and we piled back into the car, his presence effectively ending further communication about the Rama plot. When Anjali started rummaging in her bag, I braced for another hottie fix-up.

Instead, she pulled out a snack bag. "*Sev?*"

"No thanks." The refusal was barely out of my mouth before she popped the fine, crunchy, deep-fried strands of chickpea dough into hers. By the time she finished the bag we'd arrived at our next stop, the biggest train station I'd ever seen.

I should stop pestering her and drop the subject of the Ramas, but the tidbits she'd revealed had only served to rattle me and I needed reassurance.

As we left the car, I tapped her on the shoulder. "Auntie, I'm a little concerned."

"About?"

"Meeting the Ramas." How to phrase this without getting her riled? "If Anu's so shrewd, won't she see through me?" And worse, reenact some of that throat-slitting action Anjali had mimed.

"We won't fail." Anjali squared her shoulders, ready for battle. "If she tries to intimidate you or harass you, she'll have me to deal with, the sneaky snake. She's a ghastly, horrid—"

"This place is still functional, Auntie?" I'd had enough of Anjali's adjectives. I got it. She hated Anu's guts and further questioning would only contribute to her blood pressure skyrocketing if the ugly puce staining her cheeks and sweat beads rolling down her forehead were any indication. Besides, the more wound up she got, the more I wondered what the hell I'd become embroiled in. If Anu discovered my treachery... I suppressed a shudder.

Anjali took a deep breath and exhaled, hopefully purging her angst. "Yes. Very busy place and the second UNESCO World Heritage site." She dabbed at the corners of her mouth and dusted off her hands. "Chhatrapati Shivaji Terminus was formerly known as Victoria Terminal."

My very own walking, talking encyclopedia. Goody.

"It's amazing," I said, unsure where to look first as we bid farewell to a patient Buddy again and joined the throng surging toward the station.

Grand Central in NYC might be impressive but this place was something else entirely. A staggering feat of architecture, the station had countless archways and spires and domes and clocks that were an astounding combination of neo-Gothic, early Victorian, and traditional Indian.

As we entered, Anjali pointed to a platform. "Over one thousand trains pass through here daily. Efficient, yes?"

I nodded. "How many passengers?"

"About three million." She said it so casually, I could've mistaken it for 3,000.

"Wow, this place is incredible."

We strolled through the station, admiring the architecture, the wood carvings, brass railings, ornamental iron, and precise detail engraved into every stone.

As we neared the entrance, Anjali touched an archway with reverence. "So sad, the smog and acid rain is damaging this beauty." I had to agree.

"Next stop, my favorite restaurant." Anjali rubbed her hands together in glee while my stomach rolled over in revolt.

I didn't dare ask why we'd skipped seeing Ghandi's home. I knew. She'd been so rattled by my less-than-subtle harping about Anu, she needed to comfort eat. Besides, getting into a car here was living dangerously. Getting between Anjali and her apparent love of food? I wasn't that brave. "Restaurant?"

"No tour is complete without a stop at Chowpatty Beach."

A beach? Good, maybe I could walk off the inevitable gormandizing.

We made small-talk as Buddy commandeered the streets, dodging buses belching diesel fume and carts and people, so many people. Interestingly, my death grip on the seat had loosened considerably by the time we reached the beach. I must've been growing accustomed to the chaos.

Anjali gestured toward the shore. "Now we eat."

We abandoned Buddy and headed for the sand, the lack of restaurants confusing me.

Reading my mind, Anjali pointed to a row of street vendors lining the beach. "The best *bhel-puri* ever."

I'd never tried the renowned *chaat*, fast-food. With Anjali dragging me toward the nearest stall, it looked like I was about to.

She ordered and I watched, fascinated, as the young guy manning the stall dexterously laid out a neat row of *papadi* (small, crisp fried puris—flatbreads) and filled them with a mix of puffed rice, *sev*, onions, potatoes, green chilies, and an array of chutneys.

I may not have been hungry but the tantalizing aromas of tamarind, mango, and coriander made my mouth water.

"My treat." I paid the vendor, who gawked at Anjali as she popped three *bhel-puris* in her mouth in quick succession.

I laughed, loving her exuberance for food, more accustomed to it—even after a day—than the vendor.

"What's so funny?" she mumbled, eyeing the remaining three.

"I'm just happy to be here." I took one and shoved the other two in her direction.

"You sure?"

I nodded. "Positive."

She didn't wait, tossing the *bhel puris* in her mouth and sighing with pleasure.

That good, huh? I nibbled at mine, the instant sweet/sour/spicy explosion on my tastebuds making me want to demolish it as fast as Anjali. *Maybe I shouldn't have been so quick to pass on the others...*

Anjali grinned at what I assumed was my orgasmic expression. "We'll come back here one evening. You'll be amazed."

"By more food?"

She gestured toward the sand. "By everything. The beach is transformed with ferry and pony rides, balloon sellers, astrologers, contortionists, snake charmers, monkey-trainers, masseurs." She snapped her fingers. "You name it, this place has it. Very entertaining to people-watch."

Glancing at the smallish crowd, most of them dozing in the shade of trees, I couldn't imagine the carnival atmosphere she described. Would be well worth another visit.

Yeah, for the *bhel-puri*, too.

"Sounds great. What about tonight?"

She shook her head. "No can do. *Game of Thrones* finale."

I stifled a grin at her addiction to TV, along with food.

She rubbed her belly and winced—no great surprise considering what she'd stuffed in there. "Time to head home and rest."

Good. My mind spun with all I'd seen, and I couldn't wait to fill Rita in on the gossip.

Plus I needed to steel my nerves to meet the Ramas. My rapidly dwindling confidence had taken a hit following Anjali's disclosures about Anu.

This could get messy.

www.ingramcontent.com/pod-product-compliance
Lightning Source LLC
Chambersburg PA
CBHW030013290326
41934CB00005B/330

* 9 7 8 0 9 9 4 3 2 9 5 5 4 *